A SKETCH
OF THE
HINDUSTANI LANGUAGE

A SKETCH

OF THE

HINDUSTANI LANGUAGE

C. J. LYALL

GYAN

Published by

Gyan Publishing House
5, Ansari Road
Daryaganj, New Delhi-110002
Phone: 011-47034999, 9811692060
E-mail: books@gyanbooks.com

Distribution Network
gyanbooks.com
India, USA, Canada, UK, Australia

ISBN: 978-93-6780-538-1 (PB)

First Published, 1880

2nd Impression 2025

Printed at: Gyan Press, Delhi.

A SKETCH OF THE HINDUSTANI LANGUAGE
Author: C. J. LYALL

A SKETCH

OF THE

HINDUSTANI LANGUAGE

BY

C. J. LYALL, M.A., C.I.E.,

OF BALLIOL COLLEGE, OXFORD, AND OF THE BENGAL CIVIL SERVICE.

EDINBURGH:
ADAM & CHARLES BLACK.
1880.

PREFACE.

THE following pages were written as an article on the Hindustani language for the new edition of the *Encyclopædia Britannica*. This will explain many of their deficiencies in matter and style, the utmost conciseness of expression having been aimed at, and everything which could, in the writer's opinion, be omitted as not absolutely essential having been cut out. Even after the compression to which the article was subjected in MS., it was deemed by the Editor too detailed and minute in its treatment for insertion in the *Encyclopædia*.

Believing that the article may have some interest and utility for students of the most widely-spoken vernacular language of India, the writer gladly availed himself of the offer of the publishers of the *Encyclopædia* to issue it in a book form. It will be seen from the frequent statement of authorities that the sketch contains little original matter; and on all points connected with the history of the language the writer has been content to follow those guides who seemed to him best qualified. His own attainments are confined to such a knowledge of the language as a vernacular speech, as could be gained by constant daily use of it in eleven years of service in India, and some acquaintance with the literature both of former times and of the present day.

The article was finished in October 1879, and it has not, owing to the writer's return to India, been possible to utilize for it any authorities of later date. To those named at the end, should be added Dr A. F. R. Hoernle's *Comparative Grammar of the Gandian Languages, with special reference to Eastern Hindi*, which, however, the writer has not yet seen.

The writer's best acknowledgments are due to Dr R. Rost, Librarian of the India Office, for much kindly help and counsel in the compilation of the article.

C. J. L

HINDUSTANI LANGUAGE.

HINDUSTANI (correctly Hindostānī[1]) is the name given by Europeans to the most generally spoken and understood of the modern Aryan languages of India. According to its etymology it should designate the tongue spoken in that part of India which was called by the Mughal (Mogul) historians Hindostān, viz., the tract bounded on the N. by the Himālaya, on the E. by Bengal, on the S. by the Vindhyās or the Dakkhan, and on the W. by the Panjāb, and this region is in fact the original seat of the language. But outside these boundaries the use of Hindustani is widespread: it is very generally spoken and understood throughout Bengal, more especially by the Musalmān population in the eastern districts; it is rapidly ousting Panjābī as the vernacular of the region from midway between the Jumna and Satluj westwards; and in Gujarāt, the Nizam's territories, and Southern India generally, it is the usual language (under the name of Dakhnī) of the very numerous Muhammadan population.

---

[1] *Hindostān* is a Persian compound signifying "country of the Hindūs." The word rhymes in Persian and Urdū poetry with *dostān* and *bostān*, and the vowel of the second syllable is consequently *o*, not *u*; even the word now more generally pronounced *Hindū* should correctly be *Hindo*, and is often to be heard so pronounced in India (where the distinction between *ū* and *ō*, lost in Erān, still survives) by accurate reciters of Persian poetry. *Hindo* represents an earlier *Hindau*, being the modern Persian for the ancient *Hendava*, *i.e.*, a dweller in the country of the *hapta hindu* (Sk. *sapta sindhu*) or "seven rivers," now called, with the omission of two (probably the Saraswati and Drishadwati or Ghaggar), the Panj-āb.

Hindustani is, as has been said, rather the European than the native appellation: the various forms of the language are by native authors called by different names, and it may be doubted whether the name Hindustani is ever used except under European influence. The dialect written in the Persian character, largely stocked with Persian words and phrases, and spoken chiefly in towns and by Musalmāns or Hindūs imbued with Persian culture, is known as *Urdū*, a name said to be derived from the *Urdū-e muʿallā*, or royal military bazaar outside the fortified royal palace at Dehli. This language, when used in poetry, is called *Rekhtah* ("crumbled," "scattered," from the manner in which the vernacular is strewn with Persian importations), and when the poems are written in the special dialect of the *zanānah*, which has a vocabulary of its own, it is named *Rekhtī* (a feminine, in a diminutive sense, of *Rekhtah*). In the region to the south of the Narmadā the same language is called *Dakhnī* ("belonging to the Dakkhan or Deccan"); though also written in the Persian character, this variety of Urdū retains a much larger proportion of Indian (as opposed to Persian) words, and is altogether more archaic in its grammatical forms, than the language of the North; a certain proportion of its peculiarities must be ascribed to its separate development as the tongue of Muhammadan colonies severed for some centuries from their original country. On the other hand, that form of Hindustani which employs the Deva-nāgarī character or varieties of it, and is used chiefly by Hindūs, is denominated by Europeans *Hindī*, and by the natives generally (in its literary form) *bhāshā* (or *bhākhā*), that is, "the language" *par excellence*. *Hindī*, indeed, being merely an Arabic relative adjective from *Hind*, India, should by right be as applicable to any form of Hindustani as to the peculiar dialect of the Hindūs, and is in fact used by *native* authors in this sense.

Of Hindī (as above defined) there are many varieties, and on the boundaries of the Hindustani-speaking area it shades off almost imperceptibly into the cognate dialects. The following types are the most important:—

(1) The so-called High Hindī, which agrees in its grammatical structure with Urdū, but where the latter recruits its vocabulary

from Persian prefers to borrow from Sanskrit. So far as this represents an actually spoken dialect, it may be considered the language of the tract around Dehli, the Northern Duāb, and Western Ruhelkhand.

(2) Braj-bhākhā, the language of Braj (a district lying round the holy city of Mathurā), much used in literature even outside of its local limits.

(3) Kanaujī, the language of the Central Duāb, which holds a middle place between High Hindī and Braj-bhākhā.

(4) Māṛwāṛī, and (5) Mewāṛī, the dialects spoken respectively in Western and Eastern Rājpūtānā. On the south Māṛwāṛī slides into Gujarātī.

(6) and (7) The hill dialects of Gaṛhwāl and Kumāun, which shew affinities rather with Māṛwāṛī and Mewāṛī than with the neighbouring dialects of the plains.

(8) Nepālī, the language of Nepāl.

(9) Awadhī or Baiswāṛī, the dialect of Oudh (Awadh) and Eastern Ruhelkhanḍ.

(10) The dialects of Rīwāṅ (Rewah) and Baghelkhanḍ, south of Allahabad and the united Ganges and Jumna as far east as the Son.

(11) Bhojpurī, the dialect of Western Bihār and the conterminous districts of the North-Western Provinces.

(12) Tirhūtī or Maithilī, the language of Tirhūt

The local varieties of dialect in Hindī are as yet far from having been thoroughly investigated; only two or three of them have any literature, and in the mouths of the people the language changes, both as to form and vocabulary, every few miles. It is, however, believed that those above mentioned are the main types to which local variations may be referred; and at any rate they are the only forms as yet available for study by Europeans. The first eight may be classed together as belonging to a western, and the remaining four to an eastern group of dialects.

Besides the above named varieties of Urdū and Hindī, which are all living and spoken languages, there exist others which are now represented only by literary memorials. Such is the language of the heroic ballads of Rājpūtānā, among which are to be found some of the oldest specimens of Hindī; that of the *Bhagats* or Vaishnava religious reformers, the most important of whom, from a literary point of view, are Kabīr and Sūr-Dās; that of Tulsī-Dās, the author of the *Rāmāyan*, the most popular work in Hindī. The language of Tulsī-Dās belongs mainly to the eastern type now represented by Awadhī and Bhojpurī, and is denominated by Mr Kellogg (the chief and almost the only authority on Hindī dialects) *Old Pūrbī*; while that of Chand and the Bhagats is of the western type. Dr Trumpp, the translator of the *Ādi Granth*, has proposed to call the extinct dialects of the language *Hindūī*, which again he divides into *Old Hindūī*, comprising the specimens down to the close of the period of the Bhagats and the redaction of the *Ādi Granth* (about 1600), and *Hindūī*, comprising the speech of Tulsī-Dās and his contemporaries and followers down to about 1750. But this division, however convenient, does not appear to represent any actual sharp line of demarcation; the type of the language proceeds from archaic to modern by insensible gradations.

It has been said that few of these dialects have any literature; of most of them the systematic study has only recently begun. Urdū, with its varieties of Rekhtah and Dakhnī, counts a long roll of writers; grammars and dictionaries of it are easily accessible. High Hindī, as distinguished from Urdū, is an idiom of recent growth, owing its literary cultivation in a great measure to the influence of the educational department in Northern India, and to the development of a Hindū opposition to Muhammadan forms of expression. Of Old Hindūī the specimens accessible to Europeans are not numerous. A portion of the *Prithirāj Rāsau*, an heroic poem describing the career of the last Hindū king of Dehli, ascribed to Chand, has been published by the Asiatic Society of Bengal. The *Ādi Granth*, which embodies many valuable specimens of Old Hindūī in the poems of the Bhagats, has been partially translated into English by Dr Ernest Trumpp; the original text has recently been lithographed at Lahore, and a small portion of it has been appended by Dr Trumpp to his translation. Portions of the poems of Kabīr and his followers have been printed in India, but are seldom to be found, except in manuscript, in Europe. Of later Hindūī literature (Sūr-Dās, Tulsī-Dās, &c.) and of compositions in modern Braj-bhāshā, there are many specimens, both printed and lithographed, to be found in any bazaar in India; the best known prose work in the last named dialect is the *Rājnīti* of Lallū Lāl. Of the other Hindī dialects our knowledge is derived mainly from the grammar of Mr Kellogg (Allahabad, 1876) and the essays of Messrs Hoernle and Beames; in some of them (Nepālī, Baghelkhanḍī, and perhaps others) versions of the Bible and New Testament have been prepared under the direction of missionaries; of one, Mārwāṛī, we have a valuable specimen in a collection of *Khiyāls* or dramas edited by the Rev. J. Robson of the Presbyterian mission at Beāwar (*Mission Press*, 1866).

For the best account as yet given of the manifold dialects of Hindustani, the reader is referred to Mr Kellogg's grammar. The type represented by Urdū and its literary sister High Hindī (frequently called, for shortness, Hindī) forms the main topic of this notice, reference being made to other dialects only incidentally, and chiefly to illustrate the history of the formation of the language.

2. Though the vocabulary of Hindustani is largely recruited from Persian, and, through Persian, from Arabic, its grammar and phonetic structure are wholly of indigenous growth. To Sanskrit and Prākrit it bears the same relationship as that borne by the Romance Languages to Classical and Low Latin; and the parallel between the two lines of descent, both in phonetic degradation and the modern growth of analytic grammatical forms, is in many respects strikingly close. As in the case of the Romance Languages, little has come down to us of the earliest forms of Hindī as distinguished from Prākrit; our oldest specimens do not go further back than the 13th century, and they already show in the germ almost all the modern developments, though their general structure still bears clear marks of the recent growth of the language out of the synthetic Prākrit. These oldest specimens are, moreover (like all Hindustani literature down to very recent times), in verse, and it must remain in some degree uncertain how far peculiarities of spelling and structure are merely to be attributed to poetic licence. The very unsettled state of the orthography of Hindī, and the possibility that in the transmission of ancient works their style has been modernized, also help to make the historical study of Old Hindī a subject in which absolute certainty is difficult of attainment; and although the few original materials which we possess are of the

greatest value, perhaps the clearest light is cast upon the historical development of the language by the actually subsisting dialectic forms of Hindī and those of its sisters, Gujarātī, Panjābī, Sindhī, Marāṭhī, Bengali, and Oṛiyā.

In ancient Aryan India Sanskrit ceased at a very early date to be the vernacular speech. Already at the appearance of Gautama Buddha (about 650 B.C.) the language current in what is now Eastern Oudh and Bihār was a Prākrit, and that form of the vulgar tongue, or another nearly related, became the sacred language of the Buddhists under the name of Māgadhī or Pālī. At a later date another Prākrit, that of the south-western area corresponding to Southern Rājpūtānā and Gujarāt, became the literary language of the Jaina sect. And still more recently the dramatists of Mālwā employed a further development of the same stock as the idiom of the menial and female characters in their plays. Grammars of Prākrit, discussing minutely its relation to Sanskrit, were drawn up by Kachchāyana, Vararuchi, Hemachandra, and others; and in the different forms of the dialects known by this common name we have the beginning and development of almost all the processes which brought into being Hindī and its sister languages. In the present article an attempt is made to trace the operation of these processes, first in regard to sounds, and secondly in the grammar in the typical instances of the inflexion of the noun and the verb, in modern Hindī.

3. Native grammarians divide words into the following classes:—

1. *Tat-samas*, or "the same as that," *i.e.*, Sanskrit;
2. *Tad-bhavas*, or "of the nature of that";
3. *Deśajas*, or "country-born";

to which should be added, as a fourth class, words of foreign (almost entirely Persian) origin. *Tatsamas* are Sanskrit words used in Hindustani without any further alteration than the loss of inflexion, as *darśan*, *pitā*, *mātā*, *kṛishṇa*. *Tadbhavas* are words of Sanskrit origin which have undergone some organic change in passing over into Hindī, as *dekh-nā*, *piu*, *māī*, *kishan*, *kānh*. *Deśajas* are words of which no Sanskrit original is traceable, as *pagṛī*, *jhagṛā*, *ḍoṅgā*. Of these classes by far the largest is the second. The tatsamas are all of late adoption, and either express ideas the necessity of words for which has only recently been felt, or replace tadbhavas which have fallen into disuse. The *deśaja* element is comparatively small, and recent investigation has traced back to Sanskrit, through Prākrit, a very large proportion of the words formerly entered in this class. The oldest literary memorials abound with tadbhavas to the exclusion of tatsamas, while the proportion of the latter is largest in modern prose works on religion, science, and the like. To the tadbhavas consequently we must look for the history of the language.

But tadbhavas, again, are of different degrees of phonetic modification as compared with Sanskrit. They fall into two classes :—(1) those which agree with the form which the Sanskrit word takes in Prākrit, and (2) those which retain something which Prākrit had rejected. Thus, of the first class we have such words as *rāu* (Pk. *rāā*, Sk. *rājā*), *sab* (Pk. *sabba*, Sk. *sarva*), *kānh* (Pk. *kaṇho*, Sk. *kṛishṇah*), *mogrā* (Pk. *muggaro*, Sk. *mudgarah*), *nai* (Pk. *naī*, Sk. *nadī*), *nayar*, *ner* (Pk. *naaram*, Sk. *nagaram*) ; of the second, *rāj* (in Old Hindī for *rājā*), *sarab*, *kishan*, *mugdar*, *nadī*, *nagar*. These are instances in which both forms of the same word are found : but in a larger proportion the modern languages have no form corresponding to the Prākrit, while that which exists has nevertheless dropped or modified something of the Sanskrit ; *e.g.*, the Sk. *bhaktah* is in Pk. *bhatto*, but in Hindī *bhagat* ; Sk. *śakaṭah* is Pk. *saaḍho*, but Hindī *sagaḍ* ; Sk. *dharmah* is Pk. *dhammo*, but Hindī *dharam*. We may therefore divide tadbhavas into (1) the *early*, or those which came through Prākrit, and (2) the *late*, or those which came direct from Sanskrit after the Prākrit stage had been passed.

It is obvious that some special cause must have brought about a fresh importation direct from Sanskrit of a stock of words for which Prākrit equivalents had previously been used. Mr Beames[1] suggests with great probability that

---

[1] *Comparative Grammar of the Modern Aryan Languages of India*, vol. i. pp. 14–17.

this importation of late tadbhavas was due to the re-establishment of Brahmanism after the extirpation of the once dominant Buddhism, about the 9th or 10th century of our era, and therefore at the time when the modern Aryan vernaculars were coming into being. Prākrit was the language of Buddhist literature, and would thus share the fate of the faith it expressed; the revival of Sanskrit learning which accompanied the re-establishment of the brahmanical creed would lead, as within the last fifty years it has again led, to the use of Sanskrit in preference to Prākrit forms; and finally, the extreme degree to which the rejection of unsupported consonants had been carried in Prākrit, and the consequent confusion in the form of many words, would make welcome a change which effected greater clearness and robustness in speech.

The foreign element is sometimes described as Persian *and* Arabic; but no borrowing direct from the latter language has ever taken place in Hindustani. Of the Arabic words in Indian tongues generally (except possibly in Sindhī) it may be said—"nihil est in Indicâ linguâ quod non prius erat in Persicâ." Such words are pronounced in India with the modifications (if any) already introduced in Persian, and not as by natives of Arabia; and where they have acquired a special and non-Arabic sense in the former language, they retain it in Hindustani. Persian was early overrun by Arabic vocables, and Firdausī's great poem was a protest (and an ineffectual one) against a usage already well established rather than a specimen of the language current in his day. These words were carried together with their own speech into India by its conquerors, and soon became naturalized there. No genuine old Hindī literature is free from such importations. They abound in Chand (about 1250 A.D.), the singer of the last stand made by the native princes of the North against the invader. The verses of Kabīr (about 1500) and his followers are even more copiously stocked with them. Tulsī-Dās (about 1600), though his theme, having been already treated in the sacred Sanskrit by his predecessor Vālmīkī, supplied him with fewer occasions for their introduction, nevertheless uses them not unfrequently.[1] In the common rustic speech they are constantly heard; and, as might have been expected, all details of government and administration are uniformly expressed by them.

But though such words are freely used in the spoken vernacular and in works written in the Devanāgarī character, they are much more frequent in Urdū, where the Persian character is used, and Persian models have throughout supplied inspiration to Indian writers. In this idiom the same abuse is manifest as in the so-called High Hindī; writers, to display their learning, have rejected vernacular words of common use in favour of less known Persian terms, as in the latter recourse has been had to Sanskrit. This importation of foreign words, however, has not been altogether wanton, or the work of conquerors ignorant of the tongue of the people. On the contrary, the Urdū language took its rise in the efforts of the ever-pliable Hindū to assimilate the language of his rulers. Its authors were Kāyaṭhs and Khatrīs employed in the administration and acquainted with Persian, not Persians or Persianized Turks, who for many centuries used only their own language for literary purposes. To these is due the idea of employing the Persian character for their vernacular speech, and the consequent preference for words to which that character is native. And thus all the non-religious higher thought of the people, all that the rustic speech feels no need of expressing, naturally now finds its utterance in Persian, in the same way as French and Latin words are used in English for the same purpose. Persian is now no foreign idiom in India, and though its excessive use is repugnant to good taste, it would be a foolish purism and a political mistake to attempt (as some have attempted) to eliminate it from the Hindū literature of the day. All the sounds of the Persian language are now familiar to the people; the combinations of consonants common in Sanskrit are beyond their powers of

---

[1] It is to be noticed that these are not words expressing remote or rarely mentioned objects, but things of the commonest and most every-day sort; nor are they words for which a vernacular equivalent is wanting in Hindī. The inference, therefore, is that they were in constant daily use 600 years ago as they are now.

utterance; English is still more strange to their lips, and assumes in the written character forms which would be unrecognizable to one unacquainted with Indian phonetics.

The Persian of India, from which the Indian vernaculars have been recruited, differs in many respects, both as to sound, idiom, and vocabulary, from that now spoken in Erān. The sounds especially exhibit a more archaic form of the language. Thus the distinction between *ī* and *e* and *ū* and *o*, and the nasal *n*, or *nūn-i ghunnah*, after long vowels, the due observance of which is enjoined by the classical grammarians and essential to the prosody of all classical Persian poetry, have been retained in India, though now altogether absent from the language of Erān.

Hardly any other foreign language besides Persian has contributed to the vocabulary of Hindustani. Turkish words, notwithstanding the nationality of many of the rulers of Dehli, are singularly few; of Pukhto or Afghān there is probably not a single specimen. A small number of Portuguese words have made their way inland from the seaports; and a few English terms are gradually establishing themselves in the mouths of the people.

4. The sounds of Hindustani are essentially those of Sanskrit; some of those found in the latter tongue have, however, disappeared from the former. Thus, among vowels *ḷri*, *ḷrī*, and *ṛī* do not exist in the modern tongue, while *ṛi* is undistinguishable from *ri*, with which it is constantly assimilated in writing. *Anuswāra* and *Anunāsika* are generally confounded in writing (the sign of the former being used for both), though not in utterance; the former is rarely met with, being perhaps restricted to a few words where it occurs before *h* and *s* (as सिंह, संहार, pronounced, and often written, *singh*, *sanghār*, सिंघ, संघार).[1] *Visarga* is inaudible, though counted in prosody. Among the consonants, the cerebral letters ड and ढ have developed sounds of *ṛ* and *ṛh*, which exist side by side with the

---

[1] When this sign is merely a substitute in writing for a nasal of one of the five organs (as गंगा, पिंजरा, घंटा, दंतान, खंभा) it is not really anuswāra.

original *ḍ* and *ḍh*, and are indicated by a dot below the letters, thus—ड़ ढ़. Of the nasals, ङ and ञ are generally expressed by anuswāra, and ण is in all tadbhavas represented by न, remaining only in tatsamas, and in them even being hardly distinguished in the popular speech. फ is very generally, though not universally, pronounced as *f*. व stands midway between *v* and *w*, the former sound, or even *b*, being preferred before *i*, *ī*, *e*, *ai*, and the latter before *a*, *ā*, *u*, *ū*, *o*, *au*. In the sibilants there is some confusion; श has been generally appropriated to the sound of *sh* (as in *shall*), while ष is used to represent ख *kh*. The tendency in the vulgar speech is to use स for all the original sibilants of Sanskrit and for the Persian *sh* ش.[1]

In foreign words the vulgar speech replaces the Persian and Arabic consonants by the nearest indigenous equivalents. ث, ص, and س are all rendered by स; ح and ه by ह; ت and ط by त; ز, ذ, ض, and ظ by ज;[2] غ by ग; ق by क and sometimes ख (as बखत for وقت); خ by ख

[1] In this article the usual system of transliteration is followed in the vowels; in the consonants, no distinction has been made between ङ, ञ, and न, as the first two are never found except in conjunction with the tenuis, medial, or aspirates of their respective *vargas*. ण has been rendered by *ṇ*, anuswāra where medial by *ṉ*, where final (in Sanskrit and Prākrit words) by *m*, and anunāsika by *ñ*. The writer would have preferred to indicate the last by the means adopted in Portuguese, as in *João*; but as the nasalization affects both long and short vowels, this method would interfere with the diacritical marks indicating length. In Sanskrit words श is represented by *ś*, in Hindī words by *sh*. ष is in Sanskrit words *sh*; in Hindī it does not occur except with the value *kh*.

[2] There are signs of a tendency in Old Hindī to express foreign *z* by *d*. Thus कागद stands for كاغذ, हादर for حاضر, हदूर for حضور, नदर for نظر, and कादी for قاضي (last four from *Granth*).

and often क (बकस for بخش). ع when initial is unheard, and when preceded by a vowel lengthens it. Nexus of consonants, when offering any difficulty, is treated as in Sanskrit tadbhavas, by separating the consonants by a short vowel. In Urdū, however, the pronunciation follows that current in Persian, and the proper sounds of ز (ذ, ض, ظ), خ, and غ, and to a less degree those of ق and ع, have become fairly naturalized in Hindostan.

The sounds of short *e* and *o*, common in Prākrit, can hardly be said to exist in Hindustani, except in the dialects; short *e* is heard in Awadhī in a few words, and elsewhere in some diminutives. Almost the only irregularity in the Hindustani vowel-system is the tendency of अ followed by ह to fall into ए; thus रहना, सहना, are almost *rehnā*, *sehnā*; فتح, صبح (with the nexus split by short *a*) are invariably *fate*, *sube*.

A full account of sound changes, as between Sanskrit, Prākrit, and Hindī, would be a complete history of the growth of the forms of the last named language out of its predecessors. For such an account the materials are still far from sufficient. The only systematic treatment of modern Indian sounds in connexion with Prākrit which has yet been attempted is contained in the first volume of Mr Beames's *Comparative Grammar*; and the following summary of the principal facts is almost entirely based on the examples there collected.

A. *Vowel Changes.*

Vowel changes in Hindī are few and of slight importance, except in connexion with change of consonants. In general the Sanskrit vowel is retained both in Prākrit and Hindī, with such modification in its quantity only as is called for by the effect of phonetic laws on the adjacent consonants. Where Prākrit has modified the Sanskrit vowel, the modification generally reappears in Hindī. There is a tendency in the latter language, more especially in the western dialects and the older speech, to substitute *i* for *a* in unaccented syllables; and the diphthongs *ai* and *au*, where original and not the result of processes due to Hindī, are regularly replaced by *e* and *o*.[1] The vowel *ṛi* is treated in two ways in the modern language: it is either dealt with as *ri*, when the *r* if preceded by another consonant is, as usual in such a position, dropped, or, as often happens

[1] *Ai* is similarly treated in loan-words: Shaikh, Husain, Sulaimān, are in Hindī pronounced Shekh, Husen, Sulemān.

with this letter, is shifted from before to after the vowel, which in this case frequently changes to *a*; or it becomes, as in Prākrit, *u*. The latter change generally, though not invariably, occurs in contact with a labial. Instances are, of *ṛi* treated as *ri*—Sk. gṛidhra, H. giddh; Sk. ghṛita, H. ghī; Sk. tṛina, H. tin-kā; Sk. vṛiśchika, H. bichchhu; Sk. śṛinga, H. siṅg; Sk. hṛidaya, H. hiyā: of the shifting of *r*—Sk. mṛittikā, H. maṭṭī (as if from martikā); Sk. vṛitti, H. birt; Sk. tṛipta, H. tirpat; Sk. gṛiha, H. ghar (through garha): of passage into *u*—Sk. vṛiddha, H. buḍḍhā; Sk. mṛita, H. muā; Sk. pitṛi, H. piu; Sk. bhrātṛijāyā, H. bhāūj; Sk. prāvṛisha, H. pāūs. A few cases occur in which, following Prākrit, Hindī has *a* for *ṛi*: as—Sk. kṛishṇa, Pk. kaṇho, H. kānh; Sk. śṛinkhala, H. sāṅkhal (Pk. has siṇkhalo, but a form saṇkhalo probably also existed); Sk. kṛita, Pk. kaa, H. kā.

Elision of initial vowels occasionally occurs in words compounded with the inseparable prepositions ati, adhi, anu, apa, api, abhi, ava, ut, and upa, and in a few other words: as—Sk. abhyantare, H. bhītar; Sk. √adhyaksh, H. jhāṅk; Sk. upavishṭah, Pk. uvaïṭṭho, H. baiṭhā; Sk. udwoḍhā, H. dulhā; Sk. araghaṭṭa, H. rahaṭ; Sk. araṇyaṁ, Pk. raṇṇam, H. ran. The treatment of final vowels will come under consideration hereafter in connexion with the declension of the noun; it will suffice here to say that Sanskrit and Prākrit long final vowels are invariably shortened in Hindī in the older language, and in the modern speech are dropped altogether.

The most marked features of Hindī in reference to vowels are (1) the dislike to hiatus which, as compared with Prākrit, it exhibits, and (2) its irregular *sandhi*. Hiatus is a special characteristic of Prākrit, where unsupported mute consonants almost everywhere fall out, and the vowels thus brought into contact remain uncombined. In the modern language this is not invariably so; if the vowels are capable of combination, they generally coalesce, or a semi-vowel is inserted; if they are heterogeneous, they remain separate, or a semi-vowel is, as in the first case, introduced. Thus:—

Sanskrit	*Prākrit*	*makes Hindī*
mukulaḥ	maülo	maul
nakulaḥ	naülo	newalā[1]
nārikelam	nārielam	nāriyal
dwiguṇaḥ	dūuṇo	dūnā
nagaram	naaram	nayar, ner
sugandhaḥ	suandho	saundhā, sondhā
rājā	rāā	rāu, rāī (for rāwa, rāya)
Madhupurī	Mahuulī	Maholī
Sūkaragrāma	Sūaraāma	Sorāṅw, Soroṅ

Sandhi of vowels, as occurring in Sanskrit, had disappeared from Prākrit; that which takes its place in Hindī is not the Sanskrit *sandhi*, but a more irregular system. Thus the combinations *a*+*i*

---

[1] In these examples the terminations in Hindī (*ā*, *ī*) are not to be regarded as representing the Sanskrit and Prākrit forms placed against them. They have a different origin, as will be seen hereafter when the declension of nouns is explained.

and *a*+*u*, resulting from *a*+*y* and *a*+*v* when the *y* and *v* are vocalized, do not as a rule form, as in Sanskrit, *e* and *o*, but *ai* and *au*: as nayan, nain; samaya, samai; sapatnī, savattī, saut; apara, avara, aur. Where in consequence of the rejection of one of two assimilated consonants in a nexus the preceding vowel is lengthened, the result is often the *guṇa*-form rather than the long simple vowel: *e.g.*, śimbā, H. sem; vilvā, H. bel; kushṭa, H. koṛh; sunṭhi, H. soñṭh; pushkara, H. pohkar, pokhar. Dissimilar vowels sometimes coalesce: as *u*+*a* into *o* in suvarnam, suaṇṇam, H. sonā, and the instances soñdhā and Soroñ above cited; *i*+*a* into *e*, as vyanga, H. beñg; dwyarddham, divaḍḍhe, diaḍḍhe, H. ḍeṛh; vyāpārī, H. bepārī.

B. *Consonantal Changes.*

Changes in consonants differ according as the consonants in question occur singly or as members of a combination. Changes in single consonants are of two kinds: (*a*) those which result from the position of the consonant in the word, whether initial, medial, or final; and (*b*) those which are irrespective of position, and depend on differences in the organ of utterance.

I. *Single Consonants.*—a. *Positional changes.* Initial consonants are generally unchanged, whether in early or late tadbhavas; in a few cases an aspirate has been thrown back from the body of the word to the first letter, as in gṛiha, ghar, duhitā, dhīyā, and there are examples of the reverse process, as bhaginī, bahin (for bhaïn).

Medial consonants are either retained, softened (the tenues to mediæ, the mediæ to semi-vowels and vowels), or disappear altogether. The cases of retention of the unaspirated letters of the five *vargas* are comparatively few, except with the cerebrals, to which the rule as to elision does not apply. च is the letter which most often survives in the modern tongue, though in Prākrit this also goes out; nasals, semi-vowels, sibilants, and *h* are generally retained. Softening is a process of which, more especially with the gutturals, cerebrals, and labials, there are many examples: kāka, kāg; kaṉkāla, kañgāl; paryaṉka, palañg; kuṉchikā, kuñjī; kaṭi, kiṛā; karpaṭa, kapṛā; kaṭāha, kaṛāh; vaṭa, baṛ; ghaṭa, ghaṛā. *P* generally passes into *v*, and often thence into *u*: *e.g.*, kapāṭa, kiwāṛ; tripāṭhi, tiwāṛī; sapādika, sawā; tāpa, tāw, tāu; śapatha (Pk. savaho) soñh; kapardda, kauṛī; sapatnī (Pk. savattī), saut. Examples of the change of *t* to *d* are rare; generally the *d* produced in Prākrit by the softening of *t* fell out before the stage was reached at which the modern language arose: thus in Pālī the 3d. pers. sing. present of verbs ends in *-adi* for the Sk. *-ati*; but in later Pk. this became *aï*, and in Hindī *ai*, *e*.

Elision is in Prākrit the general rule, and Hindī in this particular faithfully follows its parent. In the former language elision occurs with all the unaspirated gutturals, palatals, dentals, and labials, and with य and व (regarded as ज and ब). Several instances in Hindī have already been given above, and the following may be added :—

Elision of *k*: kokila, koil; suvarnakāra, sonār; kumbhakāra, kumhār (and so all nouns in -kāra indicating trades and occupations).
„ *g*: bhaginī, bahin (for bhaīn); taḍāga (Pk. talāo) talāo.
„ *ch*: sūchī, sūī; dwichatwāriṉśat, beālīs.
„ *j*: rājakulah (Pk. rāaūlo) rāwal; rājaputrah (Pk. rāaütto) rāwat; rajanī, rain; bīja, bīhan; gajendra, gaīnd.
„ *t*: pitṛi, piu; mātṛi, māī, mā; bhrātṛi, bhāī, bhāū; ghāta, ghāo; Sītā, Sīa.
„ *d*: hṛidayam, hiyā; badaram, bair, ber; kadaram (Pk. kaalam), kelā.
„ *p*: sūpakāra, suār; nāpita, nāī; dīpa, diyā; pipāsa, piās.
„ *v*: vivāha, biyāh.
„ *y*:—Ayodhyā, Awadh (for Aodh); āyah, āu.

The cerebrals are never elided; *p* and *b* are most frequently vocalized; the semi-vowels (except य and व, previously hardened so as to approach ज and ब, and then treated as those letters are), nasals, sibilants, and *h* are also very stable; *r* has dropped out in ke (conjunctive participle) for kari (anciently kai), and pai for pari (Sk. upari). The changes of the aspirated letters of the five *vargas*, which it is difficult to separate into positional and organic, will be noticed further on.

Final consonants do not, properly speaking, exist in Hindī, except in loan words from Persian; in all others the last consonant is considered to have the inherent *a*, which in poetry is commonly pronounced, though in prose it is inaudible; that, however, it was recently heard also in prose appears probable from the protection of the consonant from further change, to which as a final it would according to the general Aryan sound-laws be exposed.

b. *Organic change.* This operates without regard to position, and occasionally affects initial consonants as well as others. The guttural lenes display no tendency to organic change. There appears to be a tendency for the palatals to modulate into dentals and cerebrals, as H. choṅch and thoṅṭh from Sk. chanchu; chālis, iktālis, teṅtālīs, &c. Between the cerebrals and dentals there is much apparent confusion, and the passage of the latter into the former has been alleged to be the rule in Prākrit; this, however, from considerations adduced by Mr Beames (*Comp. Gr.*, vol. i., pp. 221–3), appears to be too wide a statement, and cases of such passage would seem to be in most instances due to special causes (generally the neighbourhood of *r*). However this may be, when the Prākrit has substituted the cerebral for the Sanskrit dental, the modern tongue generally follows it (as √pat, Pk. √paḍ, H. paṛ-nā). But a large number of words exists in which Sanskrit has the dental and Hindī the cerebral, in which the change is not found in Prākrit; while again a few cases of the reverse change occur both between Hindī and Sanskrit and within Hindī itself. The following are instances :—

Sanskrit dental = Hindī cerebral: √daṉś, H. ḍaṅk, ḍaṅs (Pk. daṉs as in Sk.); Sk. dāḍhikā, H. ḍāṛh, ḍāṛhī; Sk. √dah, H. ḍāh and dāh (Pk. dah and ḍah); Sk. dara, H. ḍar; Sk. dik, H. ḍig; Sk. √dal, H. ḍāl (Pk. dal); Sk. tilaka, H. ṭīkā (?Pk. tilao); Sk. √tan, H. tān, ṭān (Pk. taṇ, tāṇ); Sk. √dul, H. ḍolā, dolā (Pk.

ḍolā); Sk. guda, H. gāṅḍ; Sk. daṇḍa, H. ḍand, dand, ḍāṅḍ (Pk. also daṇḍa and ḍaṇḍa); Sk. dwyarddham, H. ḍeṛh (Pk. divaḍḍhe).

Sanskrit cerebral=Hindī dental: Sk. √ḍap, H. dab, dāb.

Within Hindī there is a very large number of derivatives from the Sk. √sthā (also shṭhā), in which the cerebral and dental appear to be indiscriminately used; *e.g.*, with cerebral, ṭhām, ṭhāṅ, ṭhāṅw, ṭhaur, ṭhahar, ṭhīk, &c.; with dental, thān, thānā, thal. From Sk. √truṭ we have H. ṭūṭ and toṛ. In the sister languages of Hindī there are many more instances of this interchange, and in Sindhī there is a marked preference for the cerebral where Hindī and the other languages of the group preserve the dental.

Ḍ frequently passes into *l*: *e.g.*, Sk. √krīḍ, H. khel, keli; Sk. cheṭa (softened to cheḍa), H. chelā; Sk. √pīḍ, Pk. pīl, H. pel, peṛ; Sk. taḍāga, H. talāo; Sk. shoḍaśa, H. solah: in Sk. √mṛid, Pk. mal, H. mal, the *d* has first become *ḍ* through the influence of the *r* of ṛi. A further passage of *d* into *ḍ*, and thence from *l* into *r*, is manifest in the numerals—ekādaśa, igārah; dwādaśa, bārah; trayodaśa, terah.

P in Prākrit frequently became *v* even when initial; but few instances, if any, of this change survive in modern Hindī. The archaic vai = Sk. pati is found in Chand (*Rewātaṭa*, 19, Gorī vai, "lord of the Ghorīs;" *ibid.* 25, Dakkhina vai desa, "country of the lord of the South"); but as this occurs only in compounds, it is not strictly an instance of initial *p*. Vekh-nā, from Sk. √ preksh, is rather Panjābī than Hindī.

The aspirated letters of the gutturals and dentals, as well as *bh*, regularly when medial, and sometimes even when initial, pass into *h*, losing their characteristic. The following are examples:—

kh: Sk. mukha, H. muṅh; Sk. ākheṭa, H. aheṭ.

gh: Sk. ślāghā, H. sarāh; Sk. araghaṭṭa, H. arhaṭ, rahaṭ; Sk. megha, H. meṅh; Sk. laghu, Old H. lahu.

th: Sk. śapatha, H. soṅh; Sk. gāthā, H. gāh; Sk. nātha, H. nāh; Sk. √kath, H. kah; Sk. prath-, H. pah- (in pahlā, "first," probably from Sk. prathara rather than prathama).

dh: Sk. badhira, H. bahirā; Sk. dadhi, H. dahī; Sk. sādhu, H. sāhu; Sk. krodha, H. koh; Sk. badhū, H. bahū.

bh: Sk. gabhīra, H. gahirā; Sk. ābhīra, H. ahīr; Sk. lābha, H. lāh; Sk. √subh, H. soh; Sk. √labh, H. lah, le; Sk. √bhū, H. ho; Sk. bhāṇḍa, H. hāṅḍī; Sk. bhuṇḍa, H. huṇḍī; Sk. prabhu, Old H. pahu.

This change takes place most frequently with *dh* and *bh*; with *kh*, *gh*, and *th* instances of retention are more common; it is rare at the beginning of a word, such instances occurring only with *bh* (as in bhū, bhāṇḍa, and bhuṇḍa above cited) and perhaps with *dh* (Sk. dherah = Nepālī heru; Sk. dhārakah = Hindī hārā; but these strictly speaking occur only in compounds). *Th* in some words where it is a secondary development is perhaps represented by initial h; as ho in Braj (= High Hindī thā), for thau (from sthitah): hāṅ (in mere hāṅ, uske hāṅ) from sthāne.

No instances of change in *chh* or *jh* have been found. *Ṭh* often passes into its media *ḍh*, as pīṭha, pīḍhā, √ paṭh, paṛh (and in secondary formations like kushṭha, kuṭṭho, [kūṭh] koṛh, as will be seen hereafter). *Ḍh* sometimes becomes *lh*, as in Sk. kuṭhārā [kuḍhārā], H. kulhārī (which exhibits both this change and that last mentioned); Sk. udwoḍhā, H. dulhā; Sk. udūḍhā, H. dulhin. *Ph* is generally retained, though in Prākrit it was commonly treated like *bh*; H. muktāhal, for Sk. muktāphala, seems to be an instance of the general rule.

Among the semi-vowels *l* sometimes changes to *r*, as Sk. tāla, H. tār and even tāṛ; this change is frequent in rustic and archaic Hindī, as charnā for chalnā, tarwāri for talwār, &c. The reverse change from *r* to *l*, which is almost the rule in Prākrit, is seldom found in the modern tongues; the chief example is chatwāriṉśat = chālīs. *L* also has a tendency to interchange with *n*, *e.g.*, non for lon (Sk. lavana), nāgal, nāgar, and nāñgal for Sk. lāngala; modern instances are the common word lambardār for number-dār (Anglo-Persian), noṭ and loṭ for the English (bank-) note, Nakhlau for Lakhnau. The postposition of the agent in Hindī, *ne*, has through the agency of this change been derived by some from lagi, lāgi (√lag); the forms *le* and *lāī* exist in Kumāunī and Nepālī.

Y regularly becomes *j* in Hindī at the beginning, and sometimes in the middle of a word, but more often in the latter position it is softened to *i* and combines with the adjacent vowels into a diphthong. Similarly, *v* when initial regularly becomes *b*, and when non-initial is vocalized or elided.

In the nasals Hindī does not follow the lead of the Prākrit in substituting *ṇ* for *n* (except in the Himālayan dialects and Māṛwāṛī); on the contrary, *n* regularly replaces *ṇ* in all tadbhavas, being retained only in spelling (but not in pronouncing) tatsamas. *M* (and final *anuswāra* pronounced as *m*) is treated in a very peculiar manner in a large class of words; it is resolved into a labial and a nasalization, the former being represented by *v*, often vocalized to *u*, and the latter by anunāsika; *e.g.*—

Sk. āmalaka, H. āñwlā; Sk. nāma, H. nāñw; Sk. grāma, H gāñw; Sk. śyāmala, H. sāñwlā; Sk. kumāra, H. kuñwar; Sk. kamala, H. kañwal; Sk. pādam (Pk. pāam) H. pāñw.

By this change may be explained several Hindī terminations in *-auñ*, originally Prākrit neuters in *-aam*, where the anuswāra has split up into a labial (which has been vocalized) and anunāsika. A further development is the dropping of the anunāsika, as—

Sk. nemi, H. neo; Sk. hima, H. hiw; Sk. vimāna, H. bewān; Sk. gamana, H. gaunā; Sk. chamara, H. chaurī; Sk. bāmana, H. baunā.

In some words, again, it is the labial that has been dropped:—

Sk. swāmin, H. sāīñ; Sk. dhūma, H. dhūāñ; Sk. godhūma, H. gohūñ, gehūñ; Sk. bhūmi, H. bhūīñ (anciently bhuvi).

This process is throughout peculiar to the modern languages.

It has already been said that Hindī has a tendency to substitute the dental sibilant स for श and ष; in this particular it follows the lead of Prākrit. There is also a tendency to replace the sibilant by *h*. Thus kesarī becomes keharī, pāshāna, pahān, and saptati throughout, when combined with other numerals, hattar (ik-hattar, ba-hattar, &c.); daśan similarly throughout its compounds changes its *ś* to *h*, as in Prākrit (igārah, bārah, terah, chaudah, &c.). This tendency is somewhat sparingly exhibited in Hindī; it is strongest in the western dialects bordering in Panjābī, in which language it is the rule. There are, however, several inflexional and conjugational forms common to all dialects of Hindī (especially in the oblique cases of nouns in *-ā*, in the substantive verb, and in the archaic future) which are most probably to be explained by this change, which has already set in in Prākrit. Two other changes, of limited application, must also be noticed. The first is of the sibilants into the palatals, as Sk. shash, H. chha; Sk. shashṭha, H. chhaṭṭhā; Sk. shaṭānka, H. chhaṭāṅk; Sk. śāvaka, H. chhok-ṛā. In all these instances the modern dialects follow the lead of Prākrit; one prominent instance of the change in the latter language, that of √sthā into √chiṭṭh, has, however, no representative in Hindī. In Māṛwāṛī and the Himālayan dialects, on the other hand, *ch* and *chh* frequently become *s*. The second is of ष into *kh*, which is the power generally given to this letter in late tadbhavas and tatsamas; thus Sk. bhāshā is pronounced bhākhā, Bhīshma, Bhīkham, visha, bikh, mesha, mekh, harsha, harakh, and from varsha we have both barakhnā and barasnā. Of this change Prākrit examples are wanting.

H is a stable letter in the modern tongue, and suffers no organic change.

II. *Changes of Conjunct Consonants.*—Prākrit, as a rule, suffered no dissimilar conjuncts, and in all early tadbhavas the modern languages follow its lead, though in late tadbhavas stronger principles of articulation are found. The changes which take place depend on the relative strength of the letters making up the nexus, which may with reference thereto be classified into *strong* and *weak*. The strong letters are the first four of each of the five organs, viz., क,ख,ग,घ : च,छ,ज,झ : ट,ठ,ड,ढ : त,थ,द,ध : प,फ,ब,भ. The weak letters are the nasals, semi-vowels, sibilants, and *h*, which exhibit relatively one to another different degrees of strength, but are all inferior to the strong letters. These letters may combine in the following ways:—

1. The strong nexus, formed of strong letters only;
2. The mixed nexus, formed of strong and weak letters;
3. The weak nexus, formed of weak letters only.

The immense majority of conjuncts in Sanskrit are of two consonants only; groups of three or even of four consonants occur, but rarely, and chiefly in compound or derivative words (*e.g.* tatsthāne, matsya, Lakshmaṇa); these, which almost always include a weak letter or letters, present no striking peculiarities. The weakest letter falls out, and the resulting stronger letters combine as in a conjunct of two elements. It will suffice, therefore, to confine our attention here to conjuncts consisting of two dissimilar consonants only.

The following rules for the treatment of the three kinds of nexus have been formulated by Mr Beames (*Comp. Gr.*, vol. i. pp. 281–2):—

(1) In the strong nexus the Prākrits assimilate the first letter to the last, and the modern language rejects the first of the two letters and in general lengthens the preceding vowel.

(*a*) When the second member of the nexus is an aspirate, Prākrit changes the first member into the corresponding unaspirated letter.

(*β*) When the nexus is followed by a long or heavy syllable, the modern languages do not always make the compensatory lengthening of the preceding vowel.

(2) In the mixed nexus the weak letter, whether preceding or following the strong letter, is in the Prākrit assimilated to it; and in the modern language one of the two letters is rejected, with the usual compensatory lengthening of the vowel.

(*a*) When the weak letter is a nasal and precedes the strong letter, it is changed to anuswāra in Prākrit, without, and to anunāsika in the modern language, generally with, compensatory lengthening of the vowel.[1]

(3) In the weak nexus three processes take place:—

(*a*) When the two letters are of unequal strength, the weaker is assimilated, as in the mixed nexus;

(*β*) When they are of equal or nearly equal strength, they are divided one from the other by the insertion of a vowel; or

(*γ*) They are combined into a third and different consonant.

1. The following are examples of the *strong nexus*:—

Sanskrit.	*Prākrit.*	*Hindī.*
khaḍgah	khaggo	khāg, Old H. khagga (also a late tadbhava, khaṛag)
mudgah	muggo	mūṅg
dugdhah	duddho	dūdh
mudgarah	muggaro	mogrā and mūgrā
Kanyākubja	Kaṇṇaüjja	Kanauj, Old H. Kanavajja
śabdah	saddo	sād (Old H.), sadda (Chand)
bhaktam	bhattam	bhāt
raktah	ratto	rattā (Old H.), rātā
√udgār	√uggāl	ugāl-nā
√udgam	√uggav	ug-nā
√ujjwal	√ubbal	ubal-nā
√udbhār	√ubbhār	ubhār-nā

The last four words supply examples of the sub-rule (*β*); a large number of such instances are to be found in the numerals among the derivatives of saptan, "seven."

The compensatory lengthening of the vowel in this and other cases of nexus, which is a marked feature of the modern dialects as distinguished from Prākrit, is of comparatively recent prevalence. Though cases are found as far back as our earliest specimens of Hindī,[2] in these the short vowel and doubled consonant of the Prā-

[1] The wording of this rule as given by Mr Beames has been slightly changed; in its original form it omitted to distinguish between the Prākrit anuswāra and its modern representative, the anunāsika, which are very different sounds.

[2] A few cases are even found in the Prākrit period. They are:—kāsa as well as kassa for kasya; dīham as well as diggham for dīrgham; jīhā as well as

krit are far more frequent; and in Panjābī and Sindhī the lengthened vowel is still of rare occurrence, the Prākrit form being retained. It is to be observed that the augmented vowel, being in compensation for the loss of one of two similar consonants, occurs equally in cases where the doubled consonant is original in Sanskrit, and is not the result of assimilation in Prākrit. Thus pippala is in the modern language pīpal, bhalluka bhālū, lattā lāt, lajjā lāj, &c.

2. The *mixed nexus* is more complicated in its phenomena:—*a*, nasals in a mixed nexus; *b*, sibilants in a mixed nexus; and *c*, semi-vowels in a mixed nexus.

a. *Nasals in a Mixed Nexus.*—The nasal may either precede or follow. In the first case it drops out, anunāsika is inserted, and the vowel generally lengthened in compensation for the lost consonant. Examples:—

Sk. janghā, Pk. id., H. jāṅgh; Sk. chanchu, H, choṅch; Sk. kaṇṭakah, Pk. kaṇṭao, H. kāṅṭā; Sk. suṇṭhi, H. soṅṭh; Sk. raṇḍā, H. rāṅḍ, rāṅṛ; Sk. shaṇḍah, H. sāṅḍ, sāṅṛ; Sk. chandrah, Pk. chando, H. chāṅd; Sk. √kamp, Pk. kamp, H. kāṁp-nā. The lengthening of the vowel shews that the original nasal has been lost and compensation is necessary; and the anunāsika which marks its place is a totally different sound from the nasals of full contact for which it is substituted. Apparent exceptions are—Sk. jambu, H. jāmūṅ; Sk. nimbā, H. nīm; Sk. śimbā, H. sem, where the *m* would seem to have prevailed over the stronger *b*. But it seems probable that in reality the strong letter has first absorbed the nasal (as shewn by the Gujarātī jāṁbu, Marāṭhī jāṁb), and has then been softened by the influence of the lost anunāsika into *m*.

When the nasal follows, it is assimilated to the stronger letter in Prākrit, and one of the pair is elided in Hindī, generally with compensatory lengthening of the vowel: *e.g.*, Sk. agni, Pk. aggi, H. āg; Sk. lagnah, Pk. laggo, H. lagā, lāgā; Sk. nagnah, Pk. naggo, Old H. (Chand) naggā, Mod. H. with inorganic anunāsika naṅgā. There is one combination with a following nasal which is treated in a peculiar manner: this is *jñ* ज्ञ. This conjunct, when it occurs in tatsamas and late tadbhavas, is pronounced, and sometimes written, *gy*. Thus आज्ञा is āgyā, ज्ञान, gyān; राज्ञी in Old Hindī is रागिनी rāginī, and by an analogous process यज्ञ is जाग. On the other hand, the root jñān in other derivatives becomes yān, as siyānā, ayān. In the modern language *jñ* is in two words represented by *n*, viz., rānī for rājñī, and janeo for yajñopavīta (through Pk. jannoaīo, jaṇṇoio). Lastly, in yajña and its compounds the general rule is sometimes followed, and *j* alone survives; as in Old Hindī jaj, and the common word jajmān (yajñamāna).

b. *Sibilants in a Mixed Nexus.*—When the sibilant precedes the

---

jibbhā for jihvā; isaro as well as issaro for īśwarah; rātī, rādī, and rāī as well as rattī for rātrī. The first of these is important as supplying a means of explaining the oblique bases of Hindī nouns in *-ā*, and of several pronouns.

strong letter it is commonly assimilated to it, but in the process aspirates its companion ; in Prākrit the double letter is retained, but in the modern tongue the first member goes out, and in this case the compensatory vowel-lengthening is more often than in others neglected (perhaps because in the aspirate something still remains of the lost sibilant). Examples :—

Sibilant with Guttural : Sk. skandhah, Pk. khandho, H. khāñdhā (but more commonly kāñdhā) ; Sk. pushkaram, Pk. pŏkkharam, H. pokhar ; Sk. sushkah, Pk. sokkho, sukkho, H. sūkhā.

With Palatal: Sk. paśchimah, Pk. pachchhimo, H. pachchhim; Sk. paśche (loc. of Vedic paścha), H. pāchhe ; Sk. vriśchikah, Pk. vinchhuo, H. bichchhū.

With Cerebral: Sk. drishti, Pk. ditthī, H. dīth and dīth ; Sk. mushti, Pk. mutthī, H. mūth, muthā ; Sk. kāshtah, Pk. kattho, H. kāth ; Sk. ashtan, Pk. attha, H. āth ; Sk. shashti, Pk. satthī, H. sāth ; Sk. pravishtah Pk. païttho, H, paithā.

With Dental: Sk. hastah, Pk. hattho, H. hāth ; Sk. hasti, Pk. hatthī, H. hāthī ; Sk. prastaram, Pk. pattharam, H. patthar ; Sk. pustakah, Pk. putthao, H. pothī ; Sk. mastakah, Pk. matthao, H. māthā.

With Labial: Sk. √sparś, Pk. phans, H. phañs-na ; Sk. pushpam, Pk. puppham, H. puhup, phup (for puph) ; Sk. vāshpah, Pk. vappho, H. bāph.

Occasionally, as above in pushpam = puhup, the sibilant, in passing into the aspirate, remains detached from its companion in its proper place ; another instance is *nihchai* from Sk. *niśchaya*. Should the following consonant be already aspirated, the sibilant, being unable to effect any further change in it, disappears entirely, as in the numerous derivatives of the roots √sphut, √sphat, "to burst," √sphar, √sphur, "to tremble, oscillate," and √sthā, "to stand" (in the modern languages phut, phat, phir, thā, and thā). There is a tendency for the dental in the combinations *st* and *sth* to pass into the cerebral, as is seen even in Sanskrit itself in the cognate roots √sthā and √shthā. Thus sthagah becomes thag, and asthi, Pk. atthi, has, by the throwing back of the aspirate and the softening of t into d, become haddī, hād. In many words the secondary *th* resulting from the absorption of the sibilant has, as in the last instance, been softened to *dh* ; *e.g.*, Sk. veshta, H. berhā ; Sk. kushtha, H. korh ; Sk. rushta, H. rūdh.

When the sibilant follows its companion, it passes into *chh*, and this, being a strong letter, assimilates, according to the rule for the strong nexus, the preceding mute ; *e.g.*:—

Labial with Sibilant : Sk. apsaras, Pk. achchharā, H. apchharā, apchhar, achchharī.

Guttural with Sibilant : Sk. kshuram, Pk. chhuram, H. chhurī ; Sk. kshanam, Pk. chhanam, H. chhan (also khan) ; Sk. rikshah, Pk. richchho, H. rīchh ; Sk. kshamā, Pk. chhamā, H. chhimā, Sk. Lakshmanah, H. Lachhman (also Lakkhan and Lakhan) ; Sk. Lakshmī, H. Lachchhī (also Lachhmī and Lakhī).

Dental with Sibilant: Sk. vatsah, Ph. vachchho, H. bachchhā, bachhrū; Sk. matsyah, Pk. machchho, H. machh, machchhī.

But although the result above shown from *k*+*sh* is common and regular, it is not the most usual transformation. This combination is more often changed into *kkh* and *kh*, and this in words where in Prākrit the other change (into *chchh*) had occurred. Thus:—

Sk. akshi, Pk. achchhī, is H. āṅkh; Sk. kshīram, Pk. chhīram, H. khīr; Sk. ikshu, Pk. uchchhū, H. īkh, ūkh; Sk. kshāram, Pk. chhāram, H. khār; Sk. makshikā, Pk. machchhiā, H. makkhī, mākhī (but also a diminutive, machchhar); Sk. kshetram, Pk. chhettam, H. khet, kheṛā; Sk. dakshinah, Pk. dakkhiṇo. H. dakkhin (also dahinā); Sk. pakshah, Pk. pakkho, H. pakh; Sk. drākshā, Pk. dakkhā, H. dākh.

This development is interesting, as showing that the modern languages do not invariably follow the lead of literary Prākrit, though they use Prākrit processes. It would seem that of the two results the one less used in Hindī (*ksh*=*chchh*) is the older, as exhibited in Prākrit and in several archaic dialects of Hindī where we now have *kkh*, and as more agreeable to analogy; while the change into *kkh* grew out of an inversion of which we have traces in Māgadhī Prākrit, whereby the sibilant was placed before instead of after the *k*; the combination *sk* would, as already shown, migrate into *kh*. It is also probable that the pronunciation of *kh* given to ष, which was in common use at the time when the late tadbhavas (to which class many of the words having *ksh*=*kkh* belong) were being formed, contributed to the greater prevalence in Hindī of the equivalent less used in Prākrit.

c. *The Semi-vowels in a Mixed Nexus.*—The phenomena in this combination are also of a somewhat complicated order, and it will be convenient to take first the cases in which the general rule is followed, and afterwards the apparent exceptions. Of the semi-vowels only *r* and *l* can precede a strong letter; and when that letter is a guttural, palatal, or labial, the general rule is followed with *r*, and in all cases with *l*. Examples:—

Of r *preceding*: Sk. karkaṭah, Pk. kakkaḍo, H. keṅkṛā; Sk. karkaṭikā, Pk. kakkaḍiā, H. kakṛī; Sk. mārgah, Pk. maggo, H. māṅg (Old H. magga); Sk. archi, H. āṅch; Sk. kharjūram, Pk. khajjūram, H. khajūr; Sk. mahārgah, Pk. mahaggo, H. mahaṅgā; Sk. karpaṭah, Pk. kappaḍo, H. kapṛā; Sk. karpāsam, Pk. kappāsam, H. kapās; Sk. sarpah, Pk. sappo, H. sāṁp; Sk. samarpaṇam, Pk. samappaṇam, H. samappa-nauṅ, soṁp-nā; Sk. garbham, Pk. gabbham, H. gābh; Sk. garbhinī, Pk. gabbhinī, H. gābhin; Sk. durbalah, Pk. dubbalo, H. dublā.

Of l *preceding*: Sk. valgā, Pk. vaggā, H. bāg; Sk. phālgunam, Pk. phaggunam, H. phāgun; Sk. phālgu, Pk. phaggū, H. phāg; Sk. √jalp, Pk. japp, H. jap-nā.

When the succeeding letter is a dental, the process above indicated takes place with *r* in a large number of instances:—

Sk. varttikā, Pk. battiā, H. battī; Sk. vārttā, Pk. vattā, Old H.

batta, Mod. H. bāt; Sk. karttarī, Pk. kattarī, H. katar-nī; Sk. kārttikam, Pk. kattikam, H. kātik; Sk. √kūrd, Pk. √kudd, H. kūd-nā; Sk. chaturdaśan, Pk. chaüddaha, H. chaudah.

But in the majority of cases in Prākrit a preceding *r* with a dental translates the latter into a cerebral, and this change is also exhibited in Hindī :—

r+*t* : Sk. √kart (krit), Pk. katt, H. kāt-nā; Sk. √vart (vrit), Pk. vatt, H. bāt; Sk. vartikah, Pk. vattao, H. bat-er; Sk. mrittikā, Pk. mittiā, H. mittī, mattī (where the *r* of *ri* has been thrown forward on the dental).

r+*th* : Sk. chaturthah, Pk. chaüttho, H. chauthā (in the dialects; usually chauthā).

r+*d* : Sk. kaparddah, Pk. kavaddo, H. kaurī; Sk. √tard, Pk. tadd, H. tār.

r+*dh* : Sk. vardhaki, Pk. vaddhaī, H. barhaī; Sk. vriddhah (*r* thrown forward), Pk. vuddho, H. buddhā, būrhā; Sk. sārdham, Pk. saddhe, H. sārhe.

To this list must be added instances in which the *r* of *prati* has been thrown forward to the *t*, making *parti*, which regularly appears in Prākrit as padi; in Hindī the *d*(*r*) is either retained or softened into *r*, *e.g.*—

Sk. prativāsī, Pk. padivāsī, H. parosī; Sk. pratichhāyā, Pk. padichhāā, H. parchhāīṅ.

R when the last member of a nexus with gutturals, palatals, and labials is assimilated, or when assimilation is impossible (as in initial consonants), falls out, in all early tadbhavas :—

Sk. krośa, H. kos; Sk. krodha, H. koh; Sk. chakrah, Pk. chakko, H. chakka, chāk, chakkā; Sk. vyāghrah, Pk. vaggho, H. bāgh; Sk. agre, Pk. agge, H. āge; Sk. bhratri (bhrātrikah), Pk. bhāio, H. bhāī; Sk. prastaram, Pk. pattharam, H. patthar; Sk. bhramaram, Pk. bhamaram, H. bhaṅwar.

In later tadbhavas the *r* is frequently separated from its companion and thrown forward on the next consonant; thus Sk. praśāda, pratāpa, prakāśa, pragana, pranālī become H. parsād, partāb, pargās, parganā, parnālā.

With dentals *r* as a last member likewise falls out, and frequently without effect on the organ of its companion :—

Sk. kshetram, H. khet; Sk. gotram, Pk. gŏttam, H. got; Sk. mitrah, Pk. mitto, H. mīt; Sk. gridhrah, Pk. giddho, H. giddh, gidh; Sk. rātri, Pk. rattī, H. rāt; Sk. putrah, Pk. putto, H. pūt, put; Sk. sūtram, Pk. suttam, H. sūt; Sk. dadru, Pk. daddū, H. dād; Sk. chandrah, Pk. chando, H. chāṅd; Sk. nidrā, Pk. niddā, H. nīṅd.

The change of the dental to a cerebral in such cases is not uncommon :—

Sk. chitrah, Pk. chitto, H. chīṅt (but chitrakah, chittao, chītā); Sk. patram, Pk. pattam, H. pāt; Sk. gantrī, H. gaddī, gārī; Sk. √trut, H. tūt; Sk. kshudrah, Pk. chhuddao, H. chhotā.

L following is sometimes elided, as in Sk. śukla, H. suk; but more often, both in Prākrit and Hindī, it is separated from its conjunct by an interposed vowel; *e.g.*, Sk. plīhā, H. pilhā; Sk. kleśah, Pk. kileso, H. kales; Sk. śukla, H. sukul.

Y and *v* only occur as following members, and in the immense majority of instances in combination with a dental. With letters of other organs they commonly fall out, according to rule, as: Sk. yogyah, Pk. jŏggo, H. jog; Sk. √chyū, Pk. chū, H. chū; Sk. jyoti, H. jot; Sk. pakwah, Pk. pikko, H. pakkā. In a few instances even with dentals they fall out or are vocalized, as Sk. tyāga, H. tiāg; Sk. twaritam, H. turaṅt, turt; Sk. Prithwīrāja, H. Pithorā; Sk. dwīpa, H. dīp; Sk. dwi, Pk. due, do, H. do. But with dentals generally they are raised to their higher forms of palatal and labial, and as such form a strong nexus with their companion, by which, however, they are so affected that they pass into its grade. Examples:—

T+y = ch: Sk. satyah, Pk. sachcho, H. sach, sāñch; Sk. nṛityati, Pk. nachchaï, H. nāche; Sk. mṛityu, Pk. michcha, H. mīch.

Th+y = chh: Sk. mithyā, Pk. michchhā, H. michhā.

D+y = j: Sk. adya, Pk. ajja, H. āj; Sk. vidyut, Pk. vijjulī, H. bijlī; Sk. dyūtam, Pk. jūdam, jūam, H. jūā.

Dh+y = jh: Sk. madhye, Pk. majjhe, H. majhi, māñjh; Sk. bandhyā, Pk. baṉjjhā, H. bāñjh; Sk. upādhyāyah, Pk. uajjhāo, H. ojhā; Sk. sandhyā, Pk. saṉjhā, H. sāñjh.

Of *v* changed to *b* the most numerous set of instances occurs in the numerals, where *dw* regularly becomes *b*, *e.g.*, dwādaśan, bārah; dwāviṉśati, bāīs; dwitīya, bīyā (in Chand; more commonly dūij, dūj); so also Sk. dwārah, H. bār. In combination with *t* the process has, in analogy with the changes of *y* with tenues, resulted in raising the grade of the *b* to *p*; the most common examples of this change are the reflexive pronoun āp (anciently āpu, appu) and the suffixes pan, pā, panā. The first is from Sk. ātman, Pk. appā, where the *m* has first changed into *v*, making ātvā; the second is most probably from the Sk. termination twam, twan; thus vṛiddhatwam = būṛhāpā, through buḍḍhappam. Sk. tattwa, however, appears in Old Hindī as tata, tatta. In one combination with *j*, the root √jwal, both the regular process and that usual with *d* are in force, the root becoming in Hindī both jal and bal.

3. *The Weak Nexus.*—The phenomena of this form of conjunct are complicated by the fact that among the weak letters some are stronger than others; the general rule is that the weaker yields to the stronger, as in the mixed nexus.

Nasal with Nasal.—The only forms of this in Sk. are *mn* and *nm*; the first yields no instances in Hindī; of the second Sk. janma, sanmukham, are examples, becoming in Pk. jammo, sammuham; the first word is in Hindī always a late tadbhava, janam; the second yields sāmh-nā, soṅh-iṅ.

Nasal with Semi-vowel.—In this combination the nasal generally prevails. Examples of a preceding nasal are: Sk. araṇyam, Pk. raṇṇam, H. ran; Sk. āraṇyakah, Pk. āraṇṇao, H. arnā; Sk. anya, H. ān, Old H. ani; Sk. śūnyah, Pk. suṇṇo, H. sūn, sūnā; Sk.

dhānyam, H. dhān; Sk. agamyah, Pk. agammo, H. agam (Old H. agammu); Sk. tanwinī, H. tannini (in Chand). Combinations with *l* are rare: in Sk. amlikā, H. imlī, both members survive. Examples of a preceding semi-vowel (*r*, *l*): Sk. ūrṇā, Pk. unṇā, H. ūn; Sk. karṇah, Pk. kaṇṇo, H. kān; Sk. prāghūrṇah, Pk. pāhuṇṇo, H. pāhunā; Sk. suvarṇam, Pk. suaṇṇam, sŏṇṇam, H. sonā; Sk. parṇah, Pk. paṇṇo, H. pān; Sk. chūrṇam, H. chūnā; Sk. gharmah, Pk. ghammo, H. ghām; Sk. karman, Pk. kammo, H. kām; Sk. charmah, Pk. chammo, H. chām; Sk. śālmalī, H. semal.

Nasal with Sibilant.—When the nasal precedes, it takes the form of anuswāra in Sk. and Pk., and is usually retained in the modern speech, or passes into anunāsika; as vaṉśa, baṉs, √daṉś, dañs. Of a preceding sibilant the examples show various processes in use: (1) the sibilant passes into *h*, and is placed after the nasal, which is retained—Sk. krishṇah, Pk. kaṇho, H. kānh; Sk. √snā, Pk. ṇhā, H. nhā; Sk. kaśmala, H. kumhlā-nā; (2) in a few words the aspirate has been lost—Sk. snehah, Pk. neho, H. neh; Sk. śmaśrū, Pk. massū, H. mūchh (by a vowel-change similar to that in chanchu=choñch; Sk. śmaśānam, Pk. masāṇam, H. masān; Sk. snushā, H. nūh; (3) splitting of the nexus occurs—Sk. snehah, H. saneh; Sk. smaraṇam, H. sumiran, samaran; and (4) in the following words the sibilant survives and the nasal is lost—Sk. smṛiti, H. surat (where the *u* is due to the lost nasal); Sk. raśmi, H. rās, rassā, rassī.

Semi-vowel with Semi-vowel.—The combinations of which representatives exist are *ry*, *rv*, *ly*, *lv*, *vy*, *vr*. In the nexus *ry*, *r* seems generally the stronger element, the *y* prevailing only where it passes into j:—Sk. chauryam, Pk. choriam, H. chorī; Sk. sūryyah, Pk. sūro and sujjo, H. sūr and (late tadbh.), sūraj; Sk. tūryyam, Pk. tūram, H. tūrī; Sk. kāryyam, Pk. kajjam, H. kāj; Sk. pūryate, Pk. pujjaï, H. pūj-e; Sk. āścharyyam, Pk. achchheram, H. āchijja (Chand) and acharaj (late tadbh.). In the following words a singular change takes place: Sk. paryyankah, Pk. pallaṇko, H. palaṅg; Sk. paryyāṇam, Pk. pallāṇam, H. palān, pālān. In *rv* the *v* generally becomes *b*, and as a strong letter assimilates the *r*:—Sk. sarvvah, Pk. sabbo, H. sab; Sk. pūrvah, Pk. pubbo. Old H. pubba; Sk. apūrvah, Pk. apubbo, Old H. apubba; Sk. √charv, Pk. chabb, H. chāb-nā. In late tadbhavas this nexus is always treated by splitting, as in sarab, parab (Sk. parvan, Pk. pabbo), pūrab. In the nexus *ly*, *l* prevails: Sk. kalyam, Pk. kallam, H. kāl, kal, kālh, kalh; Sk. tulyah, Pk. tullo, H. tul; Sk. maulyam, Pk. mŏllam, H. mol. In *lv* also the *l* is the stronger; perhaps the only example is Sk. vilvā, Pk. villā, H. bel. In *vy* the *v* becomes *b*, and the *y* is absorbed, or remains only as a vowel; Sk. √vyaṉś, H. bāchh-nā; Sk. vyāghrah, H. bāgh; Sk. vyatīta, H. bīt-na; Sk. vyangah H. beṅg (=biaṅg). *Vr* is treated as *br*, and the *r* is absorbed, or else the nexus is split; *r* in this nexus is usually vocalized in Sk., so that most examples are of *vṛi*—Sk. vṛikah, H. bik; Sk. vṛiddhah, H. buḍḍhā; Sk. vṛinda, H. bindā; Sk. vṛiśchikah, H. bichchhū; Sk. vrata, H. barat; Sk. vrāta, H. barāt; Sk. vraja, H.

baraj, birj (the last three words are late tadbhavas); Sk. vṛikshah, by a curious change, becomes Pk. rukkho, H. rūkh.

Semi-vowel with Sibilant.—The only semi-vowel which is found preceding a sibilant is *r* in the combinations *rsh* and *rś*. In these (1) the sibilant absorbs the semi-vowel; or (2) the nexus is split; or (3) a third dissimilar consonant results. Of the first process the following are examples: Sk. śīrshah, Pk. sisso, H. sīs; Sk. pārśwe, H. pās; Sk. √sparś, Pk. phaṇs, H. phas-nā, phañsnā; Sk. √nishkarsh (kṛish), H. nikāsnā. Of the second: Sk. varshah, Pk. bariso, H. barasnā, barsāt; Sk. sarshapam, H. sarasoñ. Of the third: Sk. √karsh (kṛish), Pk. kaḍḍh, H. kāṛhnā; Sk. √nish-karsh, Pālī nikkaḍḍh, Pk. nikkāl, H. nikāl.

The sibilant may be followed by all the semi-vowels, and in all cases proves the stronger. A following *y* is absorbed in—Sk. śyāmah, H. sām, shām; Sk. śyāmalah, H. sāñwlā; Sk. śyālah, H. sālā; Sk. avaśyāyam, H. os; Sk. pushyam, H. pūs; Sk. kaṇsyah, H. kāñsā. A following *r* is absorbed—Sk. śrī, H. sī; Sk. śrāvaṇam, H. sāwan; Sk. śriṇoti, Pk. suṇaī, H. sun-e; Sk. aśru, Pk. aṇsū, H. āñsū; Sk. śwaśru, Pk. sassū, H. sās. Late tadbhavas, however, split the nexus—Sk. śrī, H. sirī; Sk. āśrayam. H. āsarā; Sk. miśrah, H. misar; Sk. śrāvakah, H. sarāogī. A following *l* is rare; in Sk. slāghā, H. sarāh, the nexus is split. A following *v* disappears—Sk. śwaśurah, H. sasur; Sk. śwaśru, H. sās; Sk. īśwarah, Pk. issaro, H. īsar; Sk. swāmī, H. sāīñ; Sk. swaka, H. sagā: in Sk. √swap, Pālī sup, Pk. suv, H. so, and Sk. swarga, H. surag, the vowel following the *s* is due to elided *v*.

H in Sk. sometimes precedes the nasals *n* and *m*. In these cases Prākrit transposes the two, and the modern languages follow its lead—Sk. chihnah, Pk. chinho, chindho, H. chinh, chinhā; Sk. brāhmaṇah, Pk. bamhaṇo, H. bāmhan: Sk. Brahma, H. bamh, bambh, and bam.[1] Combinations of *h* with other letters are rare in old tadbhava words; it is found with following *r* under the form *ṛi* in hṛidaya and its derivatives, which in Hindī appear either as hiyā, hiya, &c., with loss of *r*, or as rid, ridā, with loss of *h*. Followed by *y* and *v*, those semi-vowels are strengthened to *j* and *v*, which *h* then aspirates. Cases of the nexus *hy* do not perhaps occur in Hindī;[2] but in the cognate Panjābī we have—Sk. guhyah, Pk. gujjho, Panj. gujjhā; Sk. vāhyakah, Pk. vajjhao, Panj. bājh, bājhoñ. Instances of *hv* are—Sk. jihvā, Pk. jibbhā, jīhā, H. jībh; Sk. vihvalah, Pk. vebbhalo, H. bihbal (late tadbh.).

5. *Grammar.*—In the following paragraphs we propose, in illustration of the historic development of Hindustani out of its predecessors, to examine in the first place the inflexion of the noun (including the adjective, and inci-

[1] Used as an exclamation in praise of Mahādeva, who is thereby identified with Brahma. See Kabīr in Trumpp's *Ādi Granth*, p. 684.

[2] It is probably in this combination that we must seek the origin of the pronominal forms, mujh, tujh. from genitives which would originally be musya, tusya, and then muhya, tuhya.

dentally the pronoun), and in the second the conjugation of the verb.

While Prākrit carries inflexion in some cases (more especially in the pronouns) further even than in Sanskrit, Hindustani, on the other hand, is mainly an analytic language. Traces of inflexion remain, however, side by side with declension by particles, in the noun and pronoun; and of the tenses of the verb, while the greater number are constructed by the help of participles, there are still some which are the direct descendants of the old synthetic tenses. As we go back in the history of Hindustani, and as we extend our view to the modern dialects and the sister languages, the area of the synthetic inflexion and tense system widens; in the earliest specimens of Hindī, while much that was preserved in Prākrit has been lost, much still survives, and the modern analytic devices have not yet come into general use. Recent investigation gives no countenance to the theory once held, that the modern dialects owe the greater part of their grammatical development to non-Aryan influence. The sphere of such influence even on their vocabulary (in the production of so-called *deśaja* words) has been found, since the sound-laws of Prākrit and the modern languages have been more thoroughly investigated, to be much less than was once supposed; and in their grammar there is, with our present light, no reason to assume the existence of any elements other than those yielded by Sanskrit and Prākrit.

THE NOUN.—The modern noun is of two genders only, masculine and feminine, the Sanskrit and Prākrit neuter having been incorporated in the former. Traces of the separate existence of neuters are found in the Hindī dialects in certain terminations having anunāsika, the representative of the ancient anuswāra characteristic of the neuter nominative; but these are not now in any other way distinguished from the masculine. Of the Indo-Aryan family, only Marāṭhī and Gujarātī still maintain the three ancient genders; and in Bengali and Oṛiyā even the distinction between masculine and feminine has disappeared. The gender of modern nouns agrees generally with that in Sanskrit. The most striking development in respect of gender in Hindustani is connected with the importations from Persian. In Persian there is no distinction of gender; but all Persian nouns received over into Hindustani have been separated into masculine and feminine according to rules which appear to have been elaborated entirely within the latter language. Thus all Persian nouns in *-ah* (whether of Aryan or Semitic origin) become masculine in Hindustani, on the analogy of the masculine termination *-ā*; on the other hand, nouns (generally Arabic) in *-at* are with one or two exceptions all feminine, probably on the analogy of the Aryan feminines in *-ati*, modern *-at*. Nouns of which the gender is not determined by termination seem to be classed according to analogy of idea with vernacular nouns.

The distinction between early tadbhava nouns on the one hand and late tadbhavas and tatsamas on the other is maintained in Hindustani in respect of form; the one class agrees with Prākrit, the other with Sanskrit. This distinction is important in reference to declension; for, as will hereafter be seen, it is only in the first class that we now find traces of the original synthetic inflexion system; the latter class, assuming in Hindī generally the form which they bear in the Sanskrit nominative (with the loss of visarga, anuswāra, and final short vowels, if any), are unchanged in the singular throughout the cases.

Modern nouns, whether old or late tadbhavas, end either in a consonant or a long vowel; no genuine tadbhava is found in Hindī in the present day with a short vowel ending, words so terminated being all tatsamas or late importations from Sanskrit. But the consonantal ending does not exhibit the form in which the first class originally came into Hindī; in poetry the inherent *-a*, no longer heard in prose, is still pronounced, so that all modern consonantally ending nouns appear in the former as terminating in short *-a*. This short *-a* is the remnant, in the case of most masculines representing original Prākrit masculines, of an older *-u*; in that of masculines representing Prākrit neuters, of an older *-am* (with anuswāra); in that of feminines, of an older *-i*, *-u*, or an original Prākrit *-ā*. The neuter gender had almost disappeared from Hindī at the date of our earliest extant specimens, and thus we find original neuters in *-am* having the old masculine termination *-u*, either by transfer from proper masculines, or produced by solution of the anuswāra into a labial vowel and anunāsika. These terminations are the result of the application to the Prākrit endings of the law, universal as between that language and Old Hindī, that a long final vowel in Prākrit is shortened in the latter speech. There is no such thing as a consonantally ending noun in Prākrit; even those bases which in Sanskrit ended in consonants (as *-at*, *it*, &c.) assume in Prākrit a vowel (as *anto*, *itā*), or drop the consonant so as to lay bare the preceding vowel; and all final vowels in Prākrit are in the nominative case of nouns long. These long vowels were shortened in Old Hindī to their inherent or related simple vowels; and in the modern tongue the short vowel is dropped, its place being taken in poetry, and at an immediate stage in prose, by short *a*, which thus does duty for all the original short vowels. Thus the Old Hindī *-u*, later *-a*, and present consonantal ending of masculines, represents an original Prakrit *-o* or *-am*; Old Hindī *-i*, present consonantal ending of feminines, represents an original Prākrit *-ī*; Old Hindī *-u*, present consonantal ending of feminines, represents an original Prākrit *ū*;

Old Hindī *-a*, present consonantal ending of feminines, represents an original Prākrit *-ā*.

The old tadbhavas which terminate in a vowel (necessarily long in present Hindī, since short final vowels have ceased to be pronounced) come into the modern tongue by a strictly analogous process. We have seen that a Prākrit long vowel ending becomes short in early and disappears in later Hindī; it follows, therefore, in order that a Hindī noun may exhibit a long vowel ending, that it must represent something *more* in Prākrit than a long vowel; and turning to the latter language we find what we are in search of. All Prākrit nouns which end in a dissyllable consisting of two vowels separated by a hiatus, *and such nouns only*, appear in Hindī with a long vowel-ending. Thus Sk. pāṇīyam, Pk. pāṇiam, is in Hindī pānī; Sk. hṛidayam, Pk. hiaam, is H. hiyā; Sk. ghṛitam, Pk. ghiam, is H. ghī; Sk. jīvah, Pk. jio, is H. jī; Sk. chauryam, Pk. choriam, is H. chorī. The most common form of the Prākrit dissyllabic ending, however, results from the addition to the simple Sanskrit stem of an augment consisting of *k* preceded by a vowel. This augment had already in Sanskrit obtained a considerable degree of prevalence; in Prākrit it might be added, and was apparently in practice added, to any noun, adjective, or participle, and even, it would appear, pronoun, whatever, without in any way affecting the sense. In *a*-stems it took in Sanskrit (in the nominative case) the forms, masculine *-akah*, feminine *-ikā*, neuter *akam*; in *i*-stems, masc. *-ikah*, fem. *-ikā*, neut. *-ikam*; in *u*-stems, masc. *-ukah*, fem. *ukā*, neut. *-ukam*. In Prākrit these terminations yield respectively *-ao*, *-iā*, *-aam*; *-io*, *-iā*, *-iam*; and *-uo*, *-uā*, *-uam*. According to the law by which long final vowels in Prākrit are shortened in Hindī, and that by which final anuswāra is resolved into *u* and anunāsika, these terminations become in the latter language, *first*, *aū*, *ia*, *aūñ*; *iu*, *ia*, *iañ*; *uu*, *ua*, *uañ*; *secondly*, owing to the modern dislike to hiatus, and by compensatory lengthening of one syllable when another is dropped, *au*, *ī*, *auñ*; *ī*, *ī*, *īñ*; *ū*, *ū*, *ūñ*; finally, *au* is further modified to *o* (Kanaujī) and *ā* (High Hindī), and the anunāsika of neuters dropped. Examples :—

Sansk.	*Sansk.*	*Prāk.*	*Old Hindī.*	*Mod. Hindī*
-akah (masc.)	kaṇṭakah	kaṉṭao	kāñṭau	kāñṭā
	ghoṭakah	ghoḍao	ghoṛau	ghoṛā
	chitrakah	chittao	chītau	chī'ā
	mastakah	matthao	māthau	māthā
-akam (neut.)	[suvarṇakam]	suaṇṇaam	sonauñ	sonā
-ikah (masc.)	vṛiśchikah	vichchhio	bichchhī	bichchhī[1]
-ikā (fem.)	makshikā	{ makkhiā machchhiā	mākhī makkhī }	makkhī
	mṛittikā	miṭṭiā	miṭṭī	miṭṭī
	karkaṭikā	kakkaḍiā	kakkaṛī	kakkaṛī, kakṛī
	kunchikā	kunjiā	kuñjī	kuñjī
-ikam (neut.)	mauktikam	mottiam	motīñ	motī
-ukah (masc.)	bhallukah	bhalluo	bhālū	bhālū
-ukā (fem.)	bālukā	bāluā	bālū	bālū
-ukam (neut.)	[aśrukam]	{ aṉsuam assuam }	āñsūñ	āñsū

[1] Nepālī form; in High H it is bichchū from a by-form in Sk. vṛiśchukah.

The above, except suvarṇakam and aśrukam, are all cases in which the *k*-augment is represented in Sanskrit; but, as already stated, its use in Prākrit was by no means confined to words in which it existed in Sanskrit: it was added, it would seem indifferently, to all nouns, substantive and adjective; and, reasoning from the forms taken in Hindī by Prākrit nouns in which it was certainly used, as proved by the (as yet far from thoroughly explored) extant specimens of Prākrit literature, we are justified in assuming that there existed a Prākrit original having this augment wherever we find Hindī nouns having those forms. Moreover, in Old Hindī, and even in a few words in the modern language, relics have survived of the process whereby *ikā* became *ī*, *ukā*, *ū*, &c. Thus we have feminines in *-iyā*, that termination being as a rule attributed to masculines (*e.g.*, būṛhiyā, kuttiyā, guṛiyā, ḍibiyā, chiṛiyā); this seems to result from arrest of the development at the Prākrit stage, when *-ikā* had become *-iā*. So we have also, from a presumable *ukah*, bhaḍuā (bhaṭukah), machhuā, pahruā, side by side with forms in *-ū* only; these are probably similar arrested developments. In poetry, more especially in the older specimens, any noun ending in *ī* or *ū* may assume the forms *-iya* and *uwa* when the metre requires it, which are exactly the intermediate forms between the Sanskrit *ikā*, *ukā* and the modern *ī*, *ū*, which analogy leads us to expect.

The foregoing rules will be found to account for all tadbhava nouns, substantive and adjective, in Hindī; that is, all such nouns of which there are representatives in Sanskrit and Prākrit. In the class of deśaja words there are similar developments; such words are comparatively few in number, and their terminations have doubtless been framed upon the analogy of the much more numerous class which have come through Prākrit. With deśaja words, however, must be classed nouns formed by means of a great variety of terminations in Hindī representing various modifications and extensions of the root-idea; as diminutives, abstract nouns, nouns of agency, and the like. It is not necessary to suppose, although the roots of such derivative words may occur in Sanskrit and Prākrit, that their modern forms came into Hindī through these languages; it is sufficient that a system of formation and inflexion was once established in the case of true tadbhavas; having been established, it naturally extended itself by analogy to all other words, whether these were part of the original old stock or later developments.

Late tadbhava and tatsama nouns, which have been taken over direct from the Sanskrit without passing through Prākrit, do not exhibit these peculiarities. They are formed by the simple process of adopting the Sanskrit nominative case, rejecting only anuswāra, visarga, and a short final *a*. Thus the Sanskrit stems ichchhā, agni, dhātu, dātṛi, mātṛi, sarit, dhanwat, rājan, nāman, mahiman, tejaswin, manas, chakshus appear in Hindī as ichchhā, agni, dhātu, dātā, mātā, sarit, dhanwān, rājā, nām, mahimā, tejaswī, man, chakshu. The only exception are bases in *-vat*, which in Hindī frequently substitute for that termination *-vant*, instead of *-vān*, as pāpwant, balwant; this is due to the influence of Prākrit, where the nom. sing. of such bases ends in *vanto*, Old H. *vantu*, later *vanta*, *vant*.

The declension of nouns is effected in Hindī by means of what are called post-positions, thus:—

Singular.

	Masc. consonantal stem.	Masc. stem in -*ā*.	Fem. consonantal stem.	Fem. stem in *ī*.
Nom.	bāgh	ghoṛā	bāt	beṭī
Accus.	{bāgh bāgh-ko	ghoṛā ghoṛe-ko	bāt bāt-ko	beṭī beṭī-ko
Dat.	bāgh-ko	ghoṛe-ko	bāt-ko	beṭī-ko
Abl.	bāgh-se	ghoṛe-se	bāt-se	beṭī-se
Loc.	bāgh-meñ	ghoṛe-meñ	bāt-meñ	beṭī-meñ
Agent	bāgh-ne	ghoṛe-ne	bāt-ne	beṭī-ne
Gen.	bāgh-kā	ghoṛe-kā	bāt-kā	beṭī-kā
Voc.	bāgh	ghoṛe	bāt	beṭī

Plural.

	Masc. consonantal stem.	Masc. stem in -*ā*.	Fem. consonantal stem.	Fem. stem in *ī*.
Nom.	bāgh	ghoṛe	bāteñ	beṭiyāñ
Accus.	{bāgh bāghoñ-ko	ghoṛe ghoṛoñ-ko	bāteñ bātoñ-ko	beṭiyāñ beṭiyoñ-ko
Dat.	bāghoñ-ko	ghoṛoñ-ko	bātoñ-ko	beṭiyoñ-ko
Abl.	bāghoñ-se	ghoṛoñ-se	bātoñ-se	beṭiyoñ-se
Loc.	bāghoñ-meñ	ghoṛoñ-meñ	bātoñ-meñ	beṭiyoñ-meñ
Agent	bāghoñ-ne	ghoṛoñ-ne	bātoñ-ne	beṭiyoñ-ne
Gen.	bāghoñ-kā	ghoṛoñ-kā	bātoñ-kā	beṭiyoñ-kā
Voc.	bāgho	ghoṛo	bāto	beṭiyo

It will be seen that in the singular one class of nouns only, the masculine in -*ā*, has a special form before the case-affixes, the other classes remaining unchanged; while in the plural three of the four, the masculine in -*ā*, the consonantally ending feminine, and the feminine in *ī*, take a special form for the nominative, and all the four take a special form before the case-affixes. These paradigms are good for all the nouns in the language; like bāgh are declined all consonantally ending masculines, and all other masculines except old tadbhavas in -*ā*; when -*ā* is a tatsama or late tadbhava ending, or the termination of a foreign word (dānā, daryā, &c.), it also follows the form of bāgh. Like ghoṛā are declined all old tadbhava masculines in -*ā* and -*āñ* (the latter retaining the nasal in the oblique singular and nominative plural); like bāt all consonantally ending feminines and all feminines in -*ā* (richā, ichchhā, &c.) which, being tatsamas, have taken over the -*ā* from the Sanskrit direct; like beṭī all feminines in -*ī* and *ū*. The few feminine nouns in -*iyā* have no special oblique form in the singular; in the plural nominative they change -*iyā* to *iyāñ*, and in the oblique to *iyoñ*, like beṭī.

In this scheme of declension there are two points to be noticed,—first, the changes in the stem, and secondly, the post-positions or case-affixes. The paradigms above given, though they represent accurately the modern High Hindī, are not identical with the ancient and dialectic forms; and it is in the latter that we must seek the processes by which the present forms were arrived at.

In the *Prithirāj Rāsau* of Chand, undoubtedly one of the oldest Hindī texts, post-positions are very sparingly used. The noun appears in a crude form, generally without any termination indicative of case or number; and the sense of a passage can be discovered only from the order of the words, and often very imperfectly even from that. Sometimes, however, the noun is inflected in the singular, and more often in the plural, by the addition of certain elements which are not the post-positions; *aha* and *ahi* are those added to the singular and nominative plural, and *ani*, *ana*, *ni*, *añ* those added to the plural. These endings seemed to be used indifferently with all the oblique cases of the singular except the vocative, and *ana*, *ani*, *añ* appear also in the plural nominative.

In the *Ādi Granth*, our second great authority for Old Hindī, we find that masculines ending in *-u* in the nominative singular end in *-a* in the oblique singular and nominative plural (as is still the case in Sindhī); masculines in *-ā* end in *-ai* in the oblique sing. and nom. plural; and both classes of nouns end in *-āñ* in the plural oblique. In the language of Kabīr and that of the *Rāmāyan* of Tulsī Dās, the same terminations as those in use in Chand are found, *-ahi*, *hi*, *aha* for the singular oblique, and *ana*, *ani*, *anha*, *anhi* for the plural.

If we turn to the pronouns, we find an oblique termination in the singular which in one class of dialects (High Hindī and other western types) is represented by *-sa*, *-su*, and in another (the southern and eastern dialects) by *-hi*. Thus, from the stem *i* (*yah*, *ih*, *e*, &c.), the oblique is in the former class *is*, *isu*, and in the latter *yāhi*, *ihi*, *yā*; from the stem *u* (*wah*, *uh*, *u*), *us*, *wāhi*, *uhi*, *wā*; from the stems *ja*, *ji* (*jo*),—*jāsu*, *jāsa*, *jis*, *jīhi*, *jāhi*; from the stem *ta*, *ti* (*so*, *to*), *tāsu*, *tāsa*, *tasa*, *tis*, *tihi*, *tā*. With the pronouns of the first and second persons singular, *hauñ* (*maiñ*) and *tū*, we find only the oblique in *h*—*mohi*, *muhi*, *mo*, and *tohi*, *tuhi*, *to*; the second type in *s* is here represented by *mujh* and *tujh*, which in all probability stand for an older *muhya*, *tuhya*, and these for *musya*, *tusya*. These inflected pronominal forms are used in old and poetic Hindī, without any further affix, for all cases except that of the agent, and sometimes even, though rarely, for that also.

From these indications and the known laws of phonetic change it appears to be a fair conclusion that the ancient *-ahi* (*-aha*, *-hi*) of the singular of nouns is identical with an older *-asi* (*-asa*, *-si*, *-su*);[1] and we are thus led to the Sanskrit genitive of *a*-stems ending in *-asya*. If we now turn to the Prākrit, we find that the Sanskrit *asya* is represented by *-assa*, *-āsa*, *āha*, and, furthermore, that this genitive of one class of Sanskrit nouns has been applied to all masculine and neuter nouns in the language. We also find that of the five Sanskrit cases (not counting the accusative and the vocative, of which the former was at an early stage in Prākrit assimilated to the nominative), the genitive termination is used to denote all except the instrumental and locative. We seem therefore to be justified in

[1] The required form *asi* to which these indications seem to point is reported by Dr Trumpp (Introduction to *Ādi Granth*, p. cxxvi.) to exist in specimens of the oldest Hindī preserved in the *Granth*. Besides the explanation of the final *-i* suggested above, it is of course also possible that it may have arisen direct from the Sk. *asya* through solution of the nexus into *asia*.

concluding that the origin of the Hindī forms in *asi*, *asa*, *ahi*, *aha* is to be found in the Sk. genitive *asya*, Pk. *assa*, *āsa*, *āha*. The *i* used interchangeably with *a* as a termination has possibly arisen from the Prākrit ablative, which in the Śauraseni dialect ends (among other forms) in *āhi*; with the tendency to fusion of case-forms which early set in in Prākrit, it was probable that two terminations so similar would be confused; and as a fact, in the Apabhranśa dialect *āhe* is used both for the ablative and genitive. There is reason also for believing that the Sanskrit termination of the locative in the pronominal declension, *-smin*, which in Prākrit became *mhin*, and was used with other than pronominal stems, has contributed to the general oblique form *-ahi*, which also appears with anunāsika, as *ahiñ*.

Applying these conclusions to our oldest specimens of Hindī, we may exhibit the development of the oblique singular hypothetically as follows:—

Masculine Nouns ending consonantally in Modern Hindī.

	Sansk.	*Prāk.*	*Early Hindī.*	*Mod. Hindī.*
Nom.	vyāghrah	vaggho	bagghu, bāghu	bāgh
Obl.	vyāghrasya	vagghassa vagghāsa vagghāha vagghāhe	bagghaha } in Chand, &c. bagghahi, &c. } baggha, bāgha, in *Granth*	bāgh

Masculine Nouns ending in -ā in Modern Hindī.

Nom.	ghoṭakah	ghoḍao	ghoṛau	ghoṛā
Obl.	ghoṭakasya	ghoḍaassa ghoḍaāsa ghoḍaāha ghoḍaahe	[ghoṛāhi] ghoṛai	ghoṛe

The oblique form ghoṛe may have arisen in another way; it was the custom of early Hindī in dealing with the Prākrit hiatus either to fuse the vowels together into one, or to separate them by a semi-vowel. So ghoḍaāha might have become either, by *sandhi*, ghoṛāha, or by insertion of *y*, ghoṛayāha, ghoṛayāh, ghoṛaya, ghoṛai, ghoṛe. This process would only affect those Prākrit nouns where the hiatus existed; that is, augmented nouns in *-akah*, the parents of the modern masculines in *-ā*; and therefore it is only in these that the oblique in *e* due to the intercalated *y* would result. That this process was that actually followed with old tadbhavas seems probable (1) from the oblique in Marāṭhī of such nouns, which ends in *-yā* (nom. ghoṛā, oblique ghoṛyā), and (2) from the fact that an Old Hindī oblique in *-āhi* as postulated above, though probable, has not actually been found. In the dialects of Rājpūtānā and the Himālaya, the oblique of masculine nouns in *-o* (corresponding to the High Hindī *-ā*) ends in *-ā*, as nom. ghoṛo, oblique ghoṛā, which would be the representative of the form resulting from *sandhi* of the hiatus, ghoṛāha. Nevertheless, the wide use of the affix *-ahi* with other than *ā*-stems seems to point to the conclusion that it must have been used with the latter also, and contributed, through ghoṛāhi, to the form ghoṛe.

Feminine nouns, whether ending in a consonant or a vowel, have lost all trace of the old inflexion in the singular; occasionally we find appended to them also in Old Hindī the affix *aha*, *ahi*, which we have been led to identify with the Sanskrit *masculine* and *neuter* genitive *asya*. This is probably due to the fact that a considerable number of nouns which in Sanskrit and Prākrit were masculines or neuters in *-i* and *-u*, have, by analogy with feminines in *-ī* and *-ū*, become feminine in Hindī. Thus *agni*, fire, is masc. in Sk. and Pk. but feminine in Hindī; *akshi*, eye, is neut. in Sk. and Pk., but fem. in Hindī; *chauryam*, Pk. *choriam*, is neut. in Sk. and Pk., but fem. in Hindī. All these nouns in Prākrit formed their genitives with *-ssa*,—aggissa, akkhissa, choriassa; which would lead, as in masculines, to the oblique termination *aha*, *ahi* in Hindī. The regular genitive of proper feminines in Prākrit was generally made by adding *-e* or *-i* to the nominative; as nom. jibbhā, bhaïnī, sassū, bāluā; genitive, jibbhāe or jibbhāi, bhaïnīe or bhaïnīi, sassūe or sassūi, bāluāe or bāluāi. The *e*, weakened to *i*, has left no survivor in Hindī, though in more Prākritic Marāṭhī traces of it are found.

In the plural, as has already been shown, the modern termination of the oblique, *oñ*, is represented in the older language by *-ana*, *ani*, *anhi*, *anha*, and in the western dialects (Nānak's Japjī, agreeing with the Rājpūtānā and Himālayan dialects of the present day) by *-añ*, *-āñ*. While in the modern speech all masculines except old tadbhavas in *-ā* have the same form in the nominative plural as in the singular, in the older dialects this termination (*ana*, &c.) is occasionally, though rarely, added to the nominative also. The anunāsika predominates in the west (to which type High Hindī belongs), the liquid *n* in the east; Braj, which stands midway, exhibits both *-ani* and *-auñ* in use together. Reasoning from the analogy of the singular, in which it has been seen that the genitive has taken possession of all the oblique cases, it seems probable that we have here the Sanskrit genitive plural of *a*-stems, *-ānām*, Pk. *-ānam*. The final *-i* of the dialectic forms possibly arose from a confusion of this termination with the nominative plural ending *-āni*, which in Sanskrit is peculiar to neuters, but in Prākrit had extended itself to masculines and feminines. In the latter termination we have probably to look for the origin of the modern feminine plural nominatives in *-eñ* (Old H. *-aiñ*) and *-iyāñ* (contracted in adjectives to *-īñ*). In Prākrit *āni* became *āī*, *aiñ*, which easily yield the present forms.

There remains for consideration only the masculine nominative plural of old tadbhavas in *-ā*, ending in *-e* (as ghoṛe, māthe, kutte). This is identical in form with the oblique singular; and it has already been noticed that in Old Hindī we find this to be the case with other nouns. In Chand we find parvataha, suraha, singhaha, &c., used for the nominative plural as well as for the singular oblique; in the fragments of Nāmdeo (about 1300) preserved in the *Granth* we have similarly bhawaraha, "bees," bhagataha, "worshippers," santaha, "saints"; and in later portions of the *Granth* (as in Nānak's Japjī, about 1500) old tadbhavas in *-u* form the nom. pl.

as well as the oblique singular in *-a* (*e.g.*, nom. sing. siddhu, pūtu, rūpu; obl. sing. and nom. pl. siddha, pūta, rūpa). Two explanations have been given of this form. The first is that of Mr Beames, who derives it from the Sanskrit nominative plural of *a*-stems, ending in *-āh*, which in Prākrit was commonly broken down to *-e*, though in some dialects *-ā* remained. So, in Hindī, while *-e* is the termination of this class of nouns in High Hindī, Braj and Kanaujī, it is *-ā* in the Rājpūtānā and Hill dialects. In Sanskrit also *-e* was the plural termination of pronominal adjectives. The second explanation is that of Dr Hoernle,[1] who, reasoning from the use in Nepālī, Bengali, and other eastern members of the Indo-Aryan family, which express plurality by adding to the oblique singular such words as *heru* (Sk. *dherah*, "multitude, heap"), *gan*, *mān*, and the like, supposes that the nominative plural was originally so formed universally, and that in those languages which do not now possess the added noun of multitude it has fallen out, leaving as a residuum the oblique singular for the nominative plural. It is difficult to decide between these two views; that such nouns of multitude are now used in Bengali and Oṛiya, which are the most abraded and least primitive members of the family, seems against Dr Hoernle's hypothesis; while on the other hand the use for the nom. plural in Old Hindī of the termination *-aha*, unexplainable on Mr Beames's theory, is in favour of it.

Other relics of ancient inflexion exist in archaic Hindī, but have for the most part disappeared from the modern tongue. The most common are locatives in *-i* and *-ai* (the last resulting from *sandhi* with final *ā* or *a*): as ghari, mani, hiyai (Chand); muhi, gharai, hukmai (Nānak), &c. Of this inflexion a modern representative exists in the Rājpūtānā dialects, which make the locatives of mascular nouns in *-o* to end in *-ai*, without any post-position, as ghoṛo, ghoṛai. Several common post-positions, as āge (Old H. aggai, Sk. agre), pīchhe (Old H. pāchhe, pāchhi, Sk. paśche), nīche, &c., are originally locatives of this form. The characteristic *-i* is the Sanskrit locative termination of *a*-stems, *-e*, which persisted in Prākrit, and was as usual shortened to *-i* in Hindī. We find ablatives in *-ahu*, *-au*, *-o*, and also in *-hi*, *-ī*, *-i*, in the Hindī of the *Ādi Granth* (as manahu, "from the mind," āpau, "from oneself," amulo amulu, "most priceless," = H. H. anmol-se anmol, jībhau, "from a tongue," muho, muhi, mukhi, "with the mouth," karamī, "by destiny," nadarī, "by a look," upadesī, "by instruction," parsādī, "by favour"). These doubtless arise from the Prākrit endings for the ablative, *-ādu*, *-āü*, *-āhe*, *-āhi*. In the pronouns the Sanskrit instrumental survives in the forms ini, in; uni, un; jini, jin; tini, tin; kini, kin (the last three corresponding to the Sk. yena, tena, kena), still used in the dialects without *ne* for the agent, and in maiṅ, taiṅ (anciently mai, tai), which are the Sk. mayā, twayā, and have been transferred in the modern language to

---

[1] *J. A. S. B.*, 1873, pt. i., p. 88, note.

the nominative, where maiñ has ousted the older hauñ (Sk. aham, with *k*-augment, ahakam, Pk. hagam, Old H. haüñ).

Much has been done of late years to clear up the nature of the post-positions, in which it was once supposed that non-Aryan influence had chiefly exerted itself. There are in Hindī three classes of words which perform the functions performed by prepositions in other languages; these are distinguished according to the manner in which they are attached to the noun they modify. The first class requires the noun to be in the oblique genitive case (ghar-ke āge, "before the house;" ghar-ke bāhir, "outside the house." The second requires it to be in the oblique, without the genitive sign *ke* (as ghoṛe-se, "from the horse;" kūeñ-meñ, "in the well"); and the third consists of words which may optionally be constructed in either way (as tāl-tale or tāl-ke tale, "below the lake;" daryā-pār or daryā-ke pār, "across the river;" us-ke bin or us-bin, "without him)." In the third class we are justified in recognizing the intermediate stage between the first and second; and in the first we find the origin of all.[1] These post-positions are, in fact, originally nouns, generally in the locative case. Thus us-ke pīchhe is literally "in the hinder part of it;" us-meñ (old forms madhi, majhi, mahi, pointing to the Sk. madhye), "in the middle of it." From this it becomes clear why the oblique form, the relic of the Sanskrit and Prākrit genitive, is used with all post-positions; and the derivation of that form from the ancient genitive receives additional confirmation. In the regular case post-positions given in the paradigm set forth above (to which others might be added), the cohesion with the noun has become so close that the genitive particle *ke* is omitted: but there was certainly a time when a genitive sense was understood to exist; thus we find in Chand *mahi*, *majhi*, &c. (modern *meñ*) and *sama* (modern *soñ*, *se*) placed before the noun, a construction only possible if the latter is conceived in the genitive. We must accordingly look to original nouns or nominal forms for the origin of all the case affixes except those of the genitive itself, which, as will hereafter be seen, have a different origin and meaning from the rest.

The *accusative* has two forms; it either agrees with the nominative, as in Prākrit, or with the *dative*, and is made by the addition of *ko* to the oblique stem. *Ko* is in Braj *kauñ*, and older forms are *kahuñ*, *kaüñ*, *kahu*, *kaü*, *ku*, *kuñ*, *kahañ*. The derivation of this word is obscure.[2] The *u* with which the word terminates in the older forms is a legitimate descendant of the Sk. anuswāra, which commonly, as already seen, separates into a labial and anunāsika.

---

[1] It is not intended to assert that all the post-positions were originally joined to the noun by the genitive particle *ke*, but that with all originally the noun was *conceived* as in the genitive, whether the case particle was used or (as almost invariably in the older language) not.

[2] Dr Trumpp deduces it from a hypothetical older *katham*, representing the Sk. *kritam*. Mr Beames would see in it the Sk. *kaksham*, accusative of *kaksha*, "armpit," the locative of which yields the Bengali *kāchchhe*, "near." This latter derivation is supported by another Old Hindī word, *pahuñ*, "near," which arises

With pronouns another word, *taiñ* (older form *tāīñ*, in Rāmānand *ṭhāi*), is used as an accusative affix, but generally with the genitive particle *ke*, though it is also found without (us-ke taīñ, us-taīñ); this is probably from the Sk. sthāne, Old H. thāni, ṭhāni. In the dialects we find, in Eastern Hindī, *ke* for the accusative and dative particle, which is also used in Bengali; this agrees with the Prākrit *kerake*, *kide*, *kade* (and, by the loss of *d*, *kae*), Sk. kṛite, which is used in late Prākrit to form a periphrastic accusative. This form is found in Chand and the *Granth*; as (P. R. xxvii. 7), Pālakāvya *kai* biraha kari anga bhae ati khīna, "Having been parted from Pālakāvya, their limbs became very thin;" and some have explained in this way the idiomatic use of *ke* in High Hindī to form possessives; as—us-ke ek betī thī, "he had one daughter." Yet another dialectic form is *nai* (Māṛwāṛī), which occurs in Chand as *naiñ*, and is the usual form in Gujarātī (*neñ*) and Panjābī (*nuñ*); in Nepālī it is *lāī*, and Mr Beames suggests that the *n* in the western forms is a substitute for *l*, and that the particle is derived from *lāgi*, *lagi*, which also yields another post-position (*lag*, *lauñ*) meaning "up to."

The *ablative* is formed in the modern tongue by *se*, which has both the senses of *with* (*i.e.*, together with, by means of) and *from*; but in the older speech *se* is restricted to the meaning *with*, while the opposite (and true ablative) sense of *from* is represented by *te*. *Se* in the dialects assumes the forms *soñ* (Braj, Bhojpurī, and Old Urdū), *sūñ*, *saū* (*Granth*), *su* (Māṛwāṛī), *sana* (Tulsī-Dās), and *sama* (Chand), as well as *setī* (Kanaujī and Japjī of Nānak). The original of the forms having anunāsika and the labial vowel is probably *sam*, the Sanskrit preposition, or more accurately, accusative of the stem *sa-*. The form *se* has arisen from *sam* by the weakening of the vowel to *i* and the solution of the anuswāra into *u* with anunāsika, yielding *siūñ*, *siu*, forms actually found in the Granth. *Sana* may be from *sange*, locative of *sanga*, which has also yielded *sang*; and *setī* from *sahita*. The other form of the ablative post-position is *te*, of which dialectic variations are *teñ* (Kanaujī, Braj, Tulsī-Dās, Chand), *tan* (Riwāī), *theñ*, *thai* (Kumāunī), *thīñ* (Bhojpurī). This word is connected by Messrs Beames and Kellogg with the Sanskrit adverbial ablative sign *-tas*, which under the form *to* had become a regular ablative termination in Prākrit. This explanation, however, fails to account for the lingual vowel, for the nasal, or for the aspirate in the dialectic forms. It may be suspected that we have here (as in *taiñ*) some derivative of the Sanskrit *sthāna*.

The *locative* is expressed by different post-positions: *meñ* in the sense of "in," *par*, "upon," *tak*, *talak* (also *tag*, *talag*), "up to," *bīch*, "in

---

from the Sk. *paksham*, accusative of *paksha*, "side": and, if the reading may be trusted, seems confirmed by a passage in Chand, xxviii. 84:—

So Prathirāja narinda
addha dinau Chāmanḍam,
adha danḍa sabba sāmanta *kachhu*
banṭi diyau Chahuvānna bar.

i.e., "Half of the ransom King Pṛithwirāj gave to Chāmanḍ Rāi: half the hero of the Chahuvāns divided among all his warriors;" where for *kachhu* other MSS. read *kahuñ* and *kaha*.

the middle of," *tale*, "below," &c. The history of most of these is sufficiently clear. *Meñ* takes in the dialects and in Old Hindī the forms *mahi*, *māñhi*, *māñhī*, *majhi*, *māñjhi*, *madhi*, &c., all of which point to the Sk. *madhye*, locative of *madhya*. *Par* is in Māṛwāṛī still *ūpari*, and dialectically *pari*, *pai*, *po*. *Ūpari* is the Sk. *upari*, which has also yielded *ūpar*. *Talak* and *tak* are apparently longer and shorter forms of the same word, and have been connected with the Sk. *daghna*, used in the same sense (by inversion *danagh*, and with change of *d* to *t*, *n* to *l*, and dropping of the aspirate, *talag*). *Lag*, *lāgi*, *lauñ*, also meaning "up to," are all descendants of the Sk. conjunctive participles *lagya* and *lagitwā* (√lag, "to be attached"), in Pk. *lagia* and *lagiūna*.

The case of the *agent* is commonly called the *instrumental*; but it has not the full range of meanings belonging to the Sk. instrumental, and is restricted to the expression of the agent in passive verbal phrases. Its post-position is *ne* in the standard dialect, Kanaujī and Gaṛhwālī, *neñ* in Braj, and *le* in Kumāunī and Nepālī. In the other dialects it does not exist, the crude oblique being used instead, or, as in Māṛwāṛī and Mewāṛī, a special oblique (in *-ai*, the usual oblique of *o*-stems being *-ā*) being employed for it. This post-position is very sparingly used in Old Hindī, and some have denied that it occurs at all in the oldest specimens; this statement, however, requires consideration. Tulsī-Dās does not use it, but his dialect is distinctly of the Eastern type, where it is still unknown.[1]

We now come to the consideration of the analytic genitive in *-kā*. It is in the first place to be observed that this case is not, properly speaking, an inflexion of the noun, but an adjective derived from it, agreeing in gender, number, and case with the noun qualified: *bāp-kā ghar* is not *patris domus*, but *paterna domus*. The Hindī adjective in *-ā* is inflected to *e* in the masculine singular oblique and throughout the plural, and to *-ī* in the feminine, both direct and

[1] The origin of this post-position has not yet been demonstrated Mr Beames would connect it with the old western accusative in *ne* or *nai* in use in the district round Dehli where the Urdū language took its origin, and he derives both from *lāgi* or *lagi*; this, however, appears to be a somewhat violent transfer of meaning. Another theory would derive it from the Sanskrit instrumental of *a*-stems, in *-ena* (purusheṇa=purush-ne); but this seems contrary to the analogy of all the other post-positions, which are independent particles (usually locatives of nouns) attached to the old genitive. *Ne* is found in Marāṭhī. the most Prākritic of the modern languages, but is there constructed, not with the crude oblique, as in Hindī, but with the genitive of the noun; thus, "by him," in Marāṭhī is *tyāchyā-neñ*, the literal equivalent of which in Hindī would be *tis-ke ne*. It appears to the present writer possible that *ne* may have arisen out of the pronominal instrumentals *ini*, *uni*, *jini*, *tini*, *kini*, which were in use down to a very recent period, and may still be heard in the dialects: the stem being recognized as *i*, *u*, *ji*, &c., the *ni* might have been conceived to be a separate particle, and its use thus extended to nouns. This process might have been facilitated by the existence (which is certain) of the other *ne* used as an accusative affix (=*ko*), with which the *-ni* in *ini*, &c., may have been supposed to be connected. The obvious convenience of such a particle would, after its use had been thus originated, lead to its general application, just as the case post-positions generally, neglected in the archaic poetry, gradually commended themselves to acceptance as aids to clearness and logical coherence, and in the present day are universally employed.

oblique, in both numbers; similarly, the genitive in *kā* takes the forms *ke* and *kī* in the same circumstances. The dialectic forms of *kā, ke, kī*, are *ko, ke, kī* in Kanaujī, *kau, ke, kī* in Braj, *ro, rā, rī* in Māṛwāṛī (and throughout Hindī in the pronouns of the first and second persons singular and plural), *ko, kā, kī* in Mewāṛī, Gaṛhwālī, and Kumāunī, with a by-form in Mewāṛī *ḷo, ḷā, ḷī.* In the Eastern dialects, the language of the Rāmāyan, and archaic Hindī, a number of forms are met with. The oldest is probably *kerā*, inflected to *kerī, kere, ker*; side by side with this we find *kara, kari*, and lastly *ka* (क), feminine *kai*. In Chand and the language of the Bhagats we find *kerā, kara, kau, ko, kā.* The discovery of the Prākrit equivalent of this particle is due to Dr Hoernle, who has shewn its existence in the *Mṛichchhakaṭi* under the forms *kelao, kerao*, which stand for *kerakah*, a Prākrit modification (with the usual *k*-augment) of the Sanskrit *kṛitah.* This element was used in Prākrit pleonastically, either with the genitive of the connected noun or with the crude form. There can be no doubt that the early Hindī *kerā* is the same as the Prākrit *kerao.* The other forms of this particle are either modifications of *kerā*, or are drawn from other forms which the Sanskrit *kṛita* assumed in Prākrit; these were *kida, kada, kaḍa, kala, kara*, and *kaa*; from one or other of which, with the *k*-augment shewn to have been added in *kelao*, can be explained all the forms taken by this particle not only in the Hindī dialects but also in Panjābī (*dā, de, dī*), Bengali and Oṛiya (*-er* and *-r*),—those forms which have not the initial *k* being the result of its elision (according to the usual phonetic law) when compounded with the noun and coming between two vowels.

THE VERB.—The conjugation of the modern Hindustani verb is extremely simple; there is but one scheme for all verbs in the language, and conjugation is effected by adding certain terminations for mood, tense, person, &c., to an unchangeable stem or root. Thus, from the root *mār*, "beat," the infinitive is *mār-nā*, the present participle *mār-tā*, the past participle passive *mār-ā*, the conjunctive participle *mār-kar*, the present *mār-ūñ*,[1] &c., the future *mār-ūñgā*, &c., the imperative *mār.* The Hindī root is thus not a grammatical abstraction, as in Sanskrit, but a significant word, which may be used by itself to denote the 2d. person singular of the imperative or the action of the verb (as—*us-ne mār khāī*, "he suffered [lit., ate] a beating"), and has in all its varieties of tense and person an easily separable and independent form.

The Verbal Stem.—In the passage of verbal forms from Sanskrit into Prākrit we have already in full operation the process which in the modern language has yielded the invariable stem. Both verbal root and conjugational apparatus are simplified; the ātmane-pada

---

[1] In this sketch this tense is called the present, because it is the legitimate descendant of the ancient Sanskrit and Prākrit present; but its use in the modern tongue is more often as a subjunctive or contingent future, though in many cases (especially in the older forms of the language) it still retains a present signification.

disappears as a separate form of the verb; the dual number is rejected; the tenses become fewer in number; and the ten conjugations of the Sanskrit are reduced to one, and that the one (the *Bhū* series) to which the great majority of the verbs in the language belong. Where in Sanskrit the root assumes an augment in the formation of the present, that augment is often incorporated into the root in Prākrit, and thus carried into formations from which in Sanskrit it is absent; *e.g.*, the root *śru* is in the 3d. sing. pres. parasmai in Sk. *śṛinoti.* which becomes in Prākrit *suṇoti*, *suṇāti* (Pālī), *suṇei* (Jaina Prākrit), *suṇaī* (Scenic Pk.); and *suṇ*, having thus been obtained as the root in Prākrit, appears in forms where in Sanskrit we should have *śru*, *śrū*, *śri*, &c.; *e.g.*, 3d. sing. pres. passive, Sk. *śrūyate*, Pk. *suṇijjaī*; past participle passive, Sk. *śruta*, Pk. *suṇia* (as if from *suṇita*). The form of the Sanskrit verb which is thus selected by Prākrit as the constant type is that of the present tense, either active or passive as the case may be; and in the reduction of the ten conjugations to one, the distinctive features of the remaining nine are either dropped or (as in the instance of √*śru* just given) incorporated into the unvarying root. In Prākrit this process is gradual, and by the succession of monuments of that group of dialects which we possess we are able to trace its development from Pālī through the Jaina to the Scenic Prākrit, in the lower varieties of the last of which it has already reached the stage which has yielded the modern Hindī verbal stems.

Only two or three conjugational developments escape this assimilating process, and that only partially; and of these exceptional formations we have remnants also in the modern languages. The first and most important of these exceptions is the past participle passive, which in a large number of verbs preserves in Prākrit (with the usual phonetic changes) the forms of the Sanskrit, and thus escapes the assimilation of the root to the form of the present tense. In the modern languages this remnant of Sanskrit conjugation appears in two forms: the past participle passive is either taken as the verbal stem and the other tenses formed from it; or the verb, while following in all other formations the general law of conformity with the Sanskrit present, possesses an anomalous past participle passive, the direct descendant of the Sanskrit and its Prākrit representative. A second exception is the passive, generally formed in Sanskrit by adding *y* to the stem before the terminations of the present ātmane-pada; in Prākrit this *y* has combined with the root, and thus formed a separate passive stem, which has survived in many cases in Hindī as a neuter verb. A third such remnant is the causal, formed in Sanskrit by adding to the vṛiddhied or gunated stem the augment *aya*, which also has representatives in Prākrit and (beside the regular causal) in Hindī.

The general process of formation of Hindī verbal stems may thus be briefly summarized. (*a*) The great majority of Hindī stems are derived from the present tense of the Prākrit active or neuter verb; but, beside these, there is (*b*) a small class in which the past participle passive, having survived in Prākrit, has been taken in Hindī as the stem; in the first class we have always to refer back the modern root to a Prākrit form conjugated on the *bhū* type, to the exclusion of other conjugations, of the Sanskrit verb. Together with the above two classes there exists (*c*) a small number of modern verbs which exhibit a double form and a corresponding active and neuter or passive sense, and which are derived, the active form from the Sanskrit present parasmai when that is active in meaning, or from the Sanskrit causal when it is not, and the neuter from the Sanskrit present parasmai when that is neuter in meaning or from the Sanskrit passive when it is not. Finally, (*d*) a limited class of verbs (only six in modern Hindī, but more in some other languages of the family and in the older dialects) have passive past participles derived, through Prākrit, direct from the Sanskrit equivalent form, and thus differing from the stem taken for all other parts of the verb. Examples of these various processes are given below :—

(*a*)

Sansk. root.	*Sansk. pres.*	*Prāk. pres.*	*Hindī pres.*	*Hindī stem.*
√bhū	bhavati	hodi, hoi	hoi, howe	ho
√chal	chalati	chalaï	chale	chal
√kamp	kampati	kampaï	kām̐pe	kām̐p
√bhram	bhramati	bhamaï	bhame, bham̐we	bham, bham̐w
√yā	yāti	jādi, jāadi, jāaï	jāe	jā
√swap	swapiti	supati, suvaï	sowe	so
√nṛit	nṛityati	nachchaï	nāche	nāch
√śak	śaknoti	sakkaṇoti	sake	sak
	śakyati	sakkaï		
√khād	khādati	khāaï	khāe	khā
√charv	charvati	chabbaï	chābe	chāb

(*b*)

Sansk. root.	*Sansk. past part. pass.*	*Prāk. past part. pass.*	*Hindī stem.*
upa+√viś	upavishṭah	uvaïṭṭho	baiṭh
pra+√viś	pravishṭah	païṭṭho	paiṭh
√pach	pakwah	pakko, pikko	pak
√śush	śushkah	sukkho	sūkh
ā+√gam	āgatah	āao	āw, ā

(*c*) Double stems,—(1) where one form of the stem has come from the active and the other from the passive of Sanskrit and Prākrit :

Root.		*Sansk. pres.*	*Prāk. pres.*	*Hindī pres.*	*Hindī root.*	
√chhuṭ	*active*	chhoṭati	chhoḍaï	chhoṛe	chhoṛ	*active*
	passive	chhuṭyate	chhuṭṭaï	chhūṭe	chhūṭ	*neuter*
√tul	*active*	tolati	tolaï	tole	tol	*active*
	passive	tulyate	tullaï	tule	tul	*neuter*
√stambh	*active*	stabhnoti	thambhaï	thām̐bhe	thām̐bh	*active*
				thāme	thām	
	passive	stabhyate	thabbhaï	tham̐bhe	tham̐bh	*neuter*
	ātmanep.	stambhate				

(2) where the neuter form is derived from the Sanskrit parasmai or ātmanepada, and the active from the Sanskrit causal :—

√sphaṭ	*parasmai*	sphaṭati	phaṭaï	phaṭe	phaṭ	*neuter*
	causal	sphāṭayati	phāḍei	phāṛe	phāṛ	*active*
√sphuṭ	*parasmai*	sphuṭati	phuṭṭaï	phuṭe	phuṭ	*neuter*
	causal	sphoṭayati	phoḍei	phoṛe	phoṛ	*active*
√tṛi	*parasmai*	tarati	taraï	tare	tar	*neuter*
	causal	tārayati	tārei	tāre	tār	*active*

(*d*) The six verbs, the past part. passive of which in Hindī exhibits a different root from that which is used in the other formations, are the following:—

honā, root *ho*, p.p.p. *huā*, *bhaā*.
marnā, " *mar*, " *muā*.
jānā, " *jā*, " *gayā*, *giyā*.
karnā, " *kar*, " *kiyā*, *kīnā*, *kīnhā*, *kīdhā* (last three archaic).
denā, " *de*, " *diyā*, *dīnā*, *dīnhā*, *dīdhā* " "
lenā, " *le*, " *liyā*, *līnā*, *līnhā*, *līdhā* " "

The processes above explained appear to be those which, either directly or by analogy, yield the great majority of Hindī primary verbal stems. These are in most cases monosyllabic, dissyllables being due either (1) to the incorporation of a Sanskrit preposition, as *utar*, *sambhāl*, *nikāl*, (2) to the formation of verbs from reduplicated roots, chiefly onomatopoetic, or (3) to the addition of a syllable to a simple root for the purpose of giving a diminutive or other modified sense to it. But besides the primary stems there are secondary ones, conjugated throughout like the primaries, which may be divided into (1) regular developments of the simple stem, as passives and causals, and (2) denominatives, or verbs formed from nouns.

Of an organic *passive* there is in the standard dialect only a single relic in what is termed the *respectful imperative.* This exists in three forms, ending respectively in *-iye*, *-iyo*, and *-iyegā* (as māriye, māriyo, māriyegā); in its modern use it is restricted to courteous forms of address, and is constructed (by a forgetfulness of its origin) as an active verb in the second singular imperative. But in the older specimens of the language, and in some peculiar phrases which have survived to modern times, we find a wider range both of forms and meanings. Thus, a very frequent use of this form of the verb in poetry (and sometimes even in prose) is to express deliberation with oneself, either in the present, imperative, or even in a future sense. A large number of instances occur in the Rāmāyan where this form can only be construed as a simple passive. We even find a present participle passive, ending in *-iyat*. So also in the common word *chāhiye*, "it is necessary," there is no precative or respectful sense; the literal meaning is—"it is wished," and in Panjābī we still have *chāhīdā hai*. In the *Granth* a fully conjugated passive formed by adding *-ī* to the simple root exists (*e.g.*, hoīai, pāīahi, bhawāīahi, jānīahi, 3d. pers. sing.; kahīani 3d. pers. plur.). In the Māṛwāṛī dialect there is still a complete form in *-īj*, as—active *karṇo*, passive *karījṇo*. All these come from the Prākrit passive, which substituted *-ia*, strengthened in some dialects to *ijja*, for the Sanskrit *y*; as Sk. śrūyate, Pk. suṇīadi, suṇīaï, suṇijjaï. Both in Sanskrit and Prākrit it was usual to employ the passive potential periphrastically, where respect was intended, for the imperative. Of the three Hindī forms *-iye* (anciently *-iyai*, *-iyahi*) is the 3d. sing. pres., *-iyo* (anciently *-iyahu*) the 3d. sing. of the imperative or potential, and *-iyegā* the 3d. sing. of the synthetic future. When the verbal stem ends in *-ī*, and sometimes when it ends in *ū*, the concourse of the vowels leads to the strengthening of *y* to *j*; *e.g.*,

√lī + iye = lījе; √jī + iye = jījе; √hū + iye = hūje. In later Hindī the origin of these forms (which are alone found in the older language) has been forgotten, and *iye*, &c., have been again added to the stem increased by *j*, as lījiye, lījiyo, hūjiye, &c.

The place of a passive in the modern language is taken by a compound verb made up of the past participle passive with *jānā*, "to go;" thus, *mārā jānā*, "to be beaten," *mārā gayā*, "he was beaten," *mārā jāegā*, "he will be beaten," &c. This form is undoubtedly ancient, being found frequently in Chand, the *Granth*, and the language of the Bhagats; but it is somewhat sparingly employed, the arrangement of the sentence being inverted so as to yield an active construction; moreover, the large number of neuter verbs with a passive sense in the language supplies to a great extent the need of a separate passive. The use of *jānā* in this manner seems to be a development peculiar to the modern languages, but it is easily intelligible; it is exactly parallel to the use of *shudan*, "to go," for the same purpose in Persian.

Causals in Hindī are of two grades, the single and the double causal. The first is made by the addition to the simple stem of the syllable *ā* (anciently and in the dialects *āw*, *āū*), and indicates that the condition implied in the simple verb is caused to exist; as *ban-nā*, "to be made," *banā-nā*, "to cause to be made, to make." The double causal is formed by adding to the simple stem the syllable *wā* (anciently and in the dialects *wāw*, *wāū*), and indicates that the condition implied in the simple causal is caused to exist; as *banā-nā*, "to make," *banwā-nā*, "to cause to make," *sun-nā*, "to hear," *sunā-nā*, "to cause to hear, to tell," *sunwā-nā*, "to cause to tell." The older form of the simple causal, in *āū*, survives in a few modern verbs as *o*, as *bhīgnā*, "to be wet," *bhigonā*, "to wet," *ḍūbnā*, "to sink (*neut.*) in water," *ḍubonā*, "to immerse." The vowel of the simple stem, if long, is regularly shortened before the causal affixes; and if the simple stem ends in a vowel, hiatus is avoided by the insertion of *l* (in the dialects *r*), as *so-nā*, *sulā-nā*; *khā-nā*, *khilā-nā*. A few verbs insert *l* (*r*) where no hiatus is possible, and in some the inserted *l* follows instead of preceding the added vowel; as *dekh-nā*, *dikh-lānā*; *baiṭh-nā*, *biṭh-lānā*, *baiṭhāl-nā*.[1] Of the first causal the origin is undoubtedly to be sought in the Sanskrit causals formed by inserting *-āp* between the guṇated or vriddhied root and the causal termination *-aya*. In Sanskrit this practice is confined to a small number of roots; but in Prākrit, owing to the disappearance of the *aya* of the regular causal (which first became *e* and then fell out altogether) and the consequent want of determinate-

---

[1] This inserted *l* or *r* is difficult to explain; it has been connected by some with the Sanskrit causal in *l*, found in a few verbs, as from √pā, causal pālayati. On the other hand, Dr Trumpp considers it to be merely euphonic, introduced to prevent hiatus; and in this view it may be parallelled by the similar insertion of *r* in Māṛwāṛī passives after stems ending in a vowel, as *leṇo*, *larīṇo*, *deṇo*, *darīṇo*. Besides the irregular forms with *l* others exist in Braj, in which the hiatus is supplied by *w*; as *khānauṅ*, *khawānauṅ*; *pīnauṅ*, *piwānauṅ*. Dikhānā, biṭhānā, sikhāna, &c., are in common use, as well as dikhlānā, biṭhlānā, sikhlānā.

ness in its form, the *āp*-form of the causal came into greatly extended use, and, *p* being as usual softened to *v*, yielded the modern forms in *āv*, *āū*, and, by dropping the junction-vowel, *ā*. The double causal is apparently a purely modern development, and is an interesting illustration of the application of analogical processes to materials acquired from the ancient grammatical stock.

Denominatives are somewhat rare, and generally take the form of the first causal; they are most numerous with reduplicated and onomatopoetic stems, and are in all probability modern growths. In their form, however, they recall the Sanskrit denominatives, which are also formed on the model of the causal in *aya*. The employment of the causal form in this process is perhaps the reason why some Hindī verbs, though causal in form, are passive or neuter in sense) as kahlānā and kahānā, "to be called"; ghabrānā, "to be agitated."

The Conjugational System.—The tenses of the Hindī verb as compared with the ancient conjugational scheme exhibit poverty in synthetic and richness in analytic and participial combinations. Of the long array of Sanskrit synthetic tenses only two survive in modern Hindī, the present and the imperative; in the older language a third, the future, is found; all the other tenses are formed analytically. The process which has yielded the present condition of things is, however, a gradual one. Even in Sanskrit itself analytical formations exist (*ūndām chakāra*, *babhūva*, and *āsa*; *bodhitā'smi*; *tena gatam*, &c.) by the side of synthetical ones; and in the successive stages of Prākrit we see the gradual disappearance of synthetic tense after tense. Where Prākrit leaves off, Hindī begins:—with a present, future, and imperative synthetically formed, and all the other tenses provided for by means of participles either with or without auxiliary verbs. In an examination of conjugational forms, therefore, our attention will be addressed first to the relics of ancient synthesis, called by Mr Beames *the simple tenses*; secondly, to *the participial tenses*, those which consist of a participle alone, or of a participle to which is attached a fragment of the old substantive verb or other auxiliary, incorporated with the participle and no longer separable from it; and thirdly, to *the compound tenses*, consisting of participles and auxiliary verbs, in which the auxiliary is still separate and distinct. The first two classes are those which are mainly found in the older forms of the language, the third being represented chiefly in the modern, where the need of fine distinctions and multiplied forms of phrase is more felt than in the archaic and poetical speech. Lastly, some verbal forms not coming within the tense system will be noticed.

a. *The Simple Tenses.*—These are, as already stated, the present (now used chiefly in a potential or contingent future sense, the imperative, and the archaic future.

The *present* has in the modern language the following terminations; *singular*, 1st pers. *-ūñ*, 2d pers. *-e*, 3d pers. *-e*; *plural*, 1st pers. *-eñ*, 2d pers. *-o*, 3d pers. *-eñ*: as—sing., 1st pers. chalūñ, 2d pers. chale, 3d pers. chale; plur., 1st pers. chaleñ, 2d pers.

chalo, 3d pers. chaleñ. If, however, we go back to the earliest monuments of the language, we find a greater variety of forms, some of which are preserved in the modern dialects. The 1st sing. ends there in *-aüñ* (as still in Awadhī and Riwāī), *-aü*, *-euñ*, and *-āñ* (the present Panjābī form); an ending in *-ī* or *-īñ* is also found (as in a fragment of Rāmānand in the *Granth*, *chālī* for *chālūñ*), which resembles the Marāṭhī and Oriyā ending in *-eñ* and the Bengali in *-i*. The 2d pers. sing. ends in our oldest specimen of Hindī in *-asi* (Jaideo, *Granth*, p. cxxiii., *ichchhasi*), which is also found in the *Rāmāyan* (jo teñ *chāhasi*; tehi na *bhajasi*), as well as a form in *-asu*; in Awadhī and Riwāī it still ends in *-as* (*māras*); a commoner form in Old Hindī is in *-ahi*, *aī*, *ai*, *i*. The 3d pers. sing. ends in *-ahi*, *aī*, *ai*, *e*, *i*, in Old Hindī, occasionally in *ehi*, *ei*, and also in *-ahu*, *-hu*, *u*. The 1st. pers. plur. ends in *-ahiñ*, *-aīñ*, in the *Rāmāyan* and the *Granth*, but in the Rājpūtānā dialects in *-āñ*, in the Himālayan dialects in *-auñ*, *ūñ*, and in Riwāī in *-an*. The 2d pers. plur. in Old Hindī always ends in *-ahu*, whence Awadhī *-aü* and Braj *-au*; in Gaṛhwālī it ends in *-ā*. The 3d pers. plur. in its oldest form ends in *-ani*, *-an*, also in *-ahiñ*, *-aīñ*; and in Gaṛhwālī it is still in *-an*. The following is a synopsis of these older forms:—

	Singular.	*Plural.*
1st pers.	aüñ, auñ, āñ, aü, eüñ, ī (īñ)	āñ, auñ, ūñ, ahiñ, aiñ
2d ,,	asi, asu, ahi, ahu. aī, ai, hi, hu, ī	ahu, aü, au. ā
3d ,,	ahi, aī, ai, ehi, ahu, -hu, ī	ani, an, ahiñ, aīñ

In Prākrit the 1st pers. sing. of the present generally keeps the Sanskrit termination *-āmi*; this is, however, in the later dialects shortened to *ami*, and corrupted to *amhi* (by confusion with the substantive verb *asmi* = *amhi*); there is also a tendency to soften the long *ā* to *e* throughout all the terminations, yielding *emi*, &c. From these forms it is not difficult to derive the Hindī terminations,—the final *-i* dropped, and the *m* separated, as usual, into *u* and anunāsika, yielding *aüñ*. The forms in *euñ*, *īñ* and *ī* seem descended from the Prākrit in *-emi*. The Prākrit 2d sing. is identical with the Sanskrit and the oldest Hindī in *-asi*; later the *s* became *h*, yielding *ahi*, *aī*, *ai*, and the modern *-e*. The 3d sing. ends in Sanskrit in *-ati*, in early Prākrit in *adi*, and in later Prākrit in *aī*: the last is one of the oldest Hindī forms. The interposed *h* was perhaps introduced merely to fill the hiatus; but there is also reason to suspect that the substantive verb (conjugated after the *bhū*-type, and yielding *asati* instead of *asti*, see *post*) had here also crept in, and that the *h* may be due, as in the 2d pers., to a converted *s*. The endings in *-u* in the 2d and 3d pers. sing. are apparently due to confusion with the imperative. The 1st pers. plural ends in Sanskrit in *-āmah*, in Prākrit in *-āmo*, *-āmu*, *-āma*, as well as in *ama*, *amu*, *amho*, *amha*, and *imo*, *imu*, which would seem to show that the Hindī forms in *auñ* and *āñ* are the oldest, those in *ahiñ*, *aīñ*, and the modern *-eñ* having arisen from confusion with the 3d plur. There is a constant tendency in the modern speech, when one person has one termination resembling that proper to another, to attribute indifferently to both the remaining terminations of each; as well as to reduce the terminations of several persons to one common form. The 2d pers. plur. ends in Sanskrit in *-atha*; but in Prākrit the ātmanepada form in *-adhwe*, and another, properly belonging to the ātmanepada imperative, in *-adhwam*, early crept into the general scheme of the tense (the ātmanepada having been lost as a separate phase of the verb), so that we have in that language the terminations *-aha*, *-adha*, *-adham*, which last yields, by the passage of *dh* into *h*, and the solution of anuswāra into anunāsika and *u*, the former of which has been lost, the archaic Hindī *ahu* and the modern *au*, *o*; the Gaṛhwālī *-ā* apparently sprang from *-aha*. The 3d pers. plur. always ends in Prākrit, as in Sanskrit, in *-anti*, which by the loss of *t* yields *-ani*, *-an*, and by the conversion of the nasal into anunāsika and its transfer to the second vowel *aiñ*, *aiñ*, *eñ*; the inserted *h* in the old forms seems to be merely an avoidance of hiatus, though it is possible here also to suppose an old *-asanti* from √*as*, yielding *ahanti*, *ahani*, *ahiñ*.

The *imperative* in the modern language does not differ from the present except in the 2d sing., which is the verbal root only, without any affix; in Old Hindī, however, we find in the 2d sing. the terminations *-esi*, *-esi*, *-asu* (*-as* in Awadhī and Riwāī) *ahi*, *-i*, *ahu*, *u*; as—mānasi, rachesi, parakhesu, karahi, sunahu, badi, taji, bhaju. The 3d sing. has the terminations *ahu*, *aü*, *hu*, *u*; the 2d plur. in Old Hindī ends in *ahu*, *ehu*, *aü*. The other persons resemble those of the present. In Prākrit we find the explanation of all these forms. The 2d sing. regularly assumed *-ahi* in place of the usual Sanskrit *-a*, extending to all conjugations the use of this termination, which is similarly used in Vedic Sanskrit, but in the classical language only in the 2d, 3d, 7th, and 9th conjugations; *ahi* shortened yielded *i*. The other forms in *esu*, *asi*, *as*, *ahu*, *u*, sprang out of the ātmanepada form, Sk. *-aswa*, Pk. *assu*, which was used in later Prākrit interchangeably with the parasmaipada. The 3d singular *aü* is pure Prākrit, for the Sk. *atu*, Pālī *adu*; *ahu* arises from *h* inserted to avoid hiatus. The other persons agree with the present, and, except the 3d plur. in *-antu*, were confounded with it as early as the Prākrit stage.

The *archaic future* is found in the present day only in Braj, Kanaujī, the Rājpūtānā dialects, and some persons of the future in Awadhī, Riwāī, and Bhojpurī; it is, however, in common use in the *Rāmāyan* and in all older Hindī poetry. There are two types of it, having for their characteristics respectively *h* and *s*; the latter is the oldest. Of the *s*-type the following is the scheme; it exists in Māṛwāṛī in the present day, and is found frequently in the *Granth*:—

		Older Type, in Granth. (Nāmdeo, Kabīr, Nānak).	*Present Māṛwāṛī.*
Sing.	1st pers.	mār-asāñ	mār-asyūñ, mār-asūñ
	2d „	mār-asahi	mār-asī
	3d „	mār-asī, -asu	mār-asī
Plur.	1st „	[mār-asahiñ]	mār-asyāñ
	2d „	[mār-asahu]	mār-asyo, mār-aso
	3d „	[mār-asahiñ][1]	mār-asī

[1] The forms in brackets are supplied from analogy, the writer not having met them in his reading.

Of the forms in *h* those of the Rāmāyan may be taken as the earlier, and those in Braj as the more modern type :—

		Rāmāyan.	*Braj.*
Sing.	1st pers.	mār-ihauñ	mār-ihauñ
	2d "	mār-ihasi, mār-ihesu / mār-ihahi, mār-iahi	mār-ihai
	3d "	mār-ihahi, mār-iahi	mār-ihai
Plur.	1st "	mār-iahiñ	mār-ihaiñ
	2d "	mār-ihahu, mār-iahu	mār-ihau
	3d "	mār-ihahiñ	mār-ihaiñ

All these forms come originally from the Sanskrit 2d future in *-ishyāmi*, *-ishyasi*, *-ishyati*, &c., which in Prākrit became *-issāmi*, *-issasi*, *-issaï*. As early as Pālī we find the characteristic *s* softened to *h* in some verbs, and in Apabhranśa we find such forms as (from √has) (1) hasihimi, (2) hasihisi, (3) hasihii; (from √kar) karihimi, karihisi, karihidi. From the Prākrits in which the *s* survived sprang the Hindī forms having that letter, and from those in which it passed into *h* the others. It is unnecessary to discuss the terminations of the several persons, as what has been said of the identical terminations of the present applies here also.

b. *The Participial Tenses.*—The ancient participles which have been adopted for conjugational purposes by the modern verb are the present active (Sk. in *-an*, *antī*, *an*), the past passive (Sk. in *-itah*, *-itā*, *itam*), and the future passive (Sk. in *-itavyah*, *-itavyā*, *-itavyam*).

The *present participle* in standard Hindī ends in the masc. in *-tā*, oblique and plur. *-te*, fem. *-tī*, plur. *-tīñ*. In the dialects and in the older language it ends in *-antu*, *ant*, *atu*, *at* for the masc., and *anti*, *ati* for the feminine, as well as in *-tau*, *-to*, *-tī*. All these forms are traceable to the Prākrit, where the terminations are *-anto*, *-antī*, *-antam*; those forms which end in a consonant or a short vowel are taken direct from the Prākrit in *-anto*, &c., while those which end in *-tā* (*to*, *tau*, *tī*) spring from a Prākrit increased form in *-antako*, *-antao*.

The present participle is used in the modern language without any affix or auxiliary to form an indefinite present, as well as a conditional past. A peculiar form occurs in the *Rāmāyan* in a past conditional sense, which has incorporated into it what we must recognize as fragments of the present of the old auxiliary √*as*. Special terminations are, however, only found in the 1st pers. sing. (*euñ*) and 2d pers. plur. (*ehu*). These terminations sometimes assume the forms *-yuñ*, *yauñ*, and *iuñ* in the 1st pers., and *eu* in the 2d plur. In the Awadhī and Riwāī dialects (which are rich in archaic conjugational forms) we find this tense conjugated throughout. Thus, from the root *ho-*, to be, we have :—

		Awadhī. Masc.	*Awadhī.* Fem.	*Riwāī.*
Sing.	1st pers.	hotyauñ	hotiuñ	hotyeuñ
	2d "	hotes	hotis	hotyes
	3d "	hot	hoti	hwāt[1]
Plur.	1st "	hoyita or hoita		hoteñ
	2d "	hotyo	hotiu	hotyen
	3d "	hote	hotiñ	hwānt[1]

[1] These forms look like remnants of quite another conjugation, the Sk.

The *past participle passive* has in Sanskrit many forms; but in Prākrit, as in other cases, so also here, the most widely used Sanskrit form, that in *-ita*, has been generally adopted as the type to the exclusion of others, and in the modern language this (with the exception of the irregular participles noticed in a former paragraph) has alone survived. *-itah* becomes in Prākrit *-ido*, *-io*, and with the *k*-augment *-iao*, which has yielded in Old Hindī, masc. *-yau* (oblique and plur. *-e*), and fem. *-ī* (plur. *-iyāñ*, *-īñ*), and in the modern language masc. *-ā*, *e*, fem. *-ī*, *-īñ*; as Sk. chalitah, Pk. chalio, chaliao, Old H. chalyau (Kanaujī and Māṛwāṛī chalyo, Kumāunī chaliyo), Mod. H. chalā. In the Old Hindī of Chand this participle is often found without the *k*-augment, terminating in *-i*, as pakari (for later pakaryau), chali (for later chalyau).

Besides the regular form in *-ā* (shortened in the Eastern dialects to *-a*) there is a widely used form of this participle which ends in *-ila*, *-ala*, as mārila, mārala. This is the form in use in Bhojpur and Tirhūt, and may be heard as far west as Allahabad. In Bengali and Oṛiyā, as well as in Marāthī and Gujarātī, it is the regular form. Its origin has been the subject of much speculation. Mr Beames and others suggest that it is a survival of an ancient form which has not been preserved in classical Sanskrit or in the written Prākrit, but is found in the Slavonic members of the Indo-European family. Some, on the other hand, have referred it to the Sanskrit *-ita* through the Prākrit forms *ida*, *iḍa*, and *ila*. But though there is no doubt that a form in *ida* existed in Prākrit, and that if a form in *iḍa* (with the cerebral *ḍ*) were found, it might pass into *-ila*, there is a want of evidence of a general transition from the dental *ida* to the cerebral *iḍa*. The only instances of which the existence is established are kiḍo from kṛitah, maḍo from mṛitah, and gaḍo from gatah; in the first two of these the *ḍ* is probably due to the elided *r*, and the third may have been formed on the analogy of the other two. Furthermore, it is to be observed that the modern representatives of *kiḍo* and *gaḍo* are not *kila* and *gala*, but *kaila* and *gaila* (in Eastern Hindi; Marāthī *kelā*, *gelā*), where the *la* appears as an addition to elements which postulate a pre-existing *kaya* and *gaya* (from *kada*, *kaa*, and *gada*, *gaa*, the hiatus filled by *y*). Some light is thrown upon this question by certain forms found in fragments by Nāmdeo and Trilochan (about 1300) preserved in the *Granth*. These ancient Hindī poets were probably from the south, and their language has affinities with Marāthī (where the *l*-form prevails), but is nevertheless still Hindī. In them we find a past participle passive in *-ialā*, contracted to *īlā* and *ilā* (as tārīale, bharīalā, ānīle, paroīle, dailā, in Nāmdeo; tājīale, pekhīale, in Trilochan); but by the side of these, and in the same fragments, we find the ordinary Hindī forms in *-ā* and *-yā* (as tare, bhae, kahe,

---

bhavati and *bhavanti*, Pk. *hoti*, *hodi*, and *hoanti*, *honti*. It is characteristic of Riwāī to turn High Hindī *o* into *wā*: as H. H. *ghoṛā*, R. *ghwāṛ*; H. H. *mo* (inflexion of hauñ, "I"), R. *mwā*; H. H. *to*, R. *twā*; so also in many other parts of this verb *ho-nā*.

dīe, jānyā, mānyā). It is evident from these that the *-la* is an augment added to a participle already formed on the type in *-ita*; and it appears to the present writer probable that this augment may be in the nature of a diminutive affix. On the one hand, *-la* is frequently used to form diminutives; thus we have machhlī by the side of māchh, bhailā in Nāmdeo = bhāī, ṭiklī dim. of ṭīkā, ghanṭālī dim. of ghanṭā, &c.; the more usual formatives for diminutives, *ṛa* and *ra*, easily interchange with *la*; and in accord with this theory we find in the *Rāmāyan* a single case of a past participle in *r* instead of *l*—*garajera* bahuri dasasīsa, "again roared the ten-headed." On the other hand, the use of this form of the past participle is prevalent, at least in the Hindī area, in exactly those tracts where in the mouths of the people every noun assumes a diminutive form (in *-uā*, *-awā*, masc., *-iyā*, fem.). That no diminutive *sense* is found in the past participle in *la* need cause no difficulty; it is an extremely common phenomenon in Hindī (and indeed in many other languages) for words that were originally diminutives to lose their special signification as such; and in Bhojpur, Oudh, and other tracts where nouns are given the diminutive ending in *-uā*, &c., there is in ninety-nine cases out of a hundred no diminutive sense implied.

In neuter verbs this participle is used as a simple past, agreeing with the subject of the sentence; as—wuh ghar-se niklā, "he went out of the house." But with active verbs a peculiar construction is adopted which is a survival from Sanskrit times. In this the participle retains its passive signification, the agent is put in its inflected case with *ne*, and the participle either agrees with the object in gender and number, or is put in the masc. sing. (the substitute for the ancient neuter), the object being in the dative. Thus "he saw a girl" is—us-ne ek laṛkī dekhī (lit., "by him a girl was seen"); "he saw the girl" is—us-ne laṛkī-ko dekhā (lit., "by him to the girl it was seen"). This construction, which is universal in the standard dialect with very few exceptions, is found throughout all the western dialects both in the early and modern examples, though in the former the use of *ne* with the agent is rare. Accordingly, the past tense thus formed can have, in active verbs, but two persons, the 3d sing. and the 3d plur. (pronouns when the object of the sentence being always constructed in the dative). In neuter verbs also, though all the persons are used, the participle suffers only the usual inflexion of adjectives in agreement with nouns, and does not otherwise vary. But in the eastern dialects generally, and also in the older language of the *Rāmāyan* frequently, a different construction is employed. In this the passive participle has become an active past tense, and agrees not with the object but with the subject of the sentence. This active use of the past participle has led, as in the case of the present participle, to the development of a regularly conjugated tense in which are incorporated fragments of the present of $\sqrt{as}$, and which is used in the active construction only. The following is the form of this tense in the Rāmāyan; modern Awadhī and Riwāī have closely corresponding forms:—

	Singular. Masc.	Fem.	*Plural.* Masc.	Fem.
1st pers.	mār-aūñ, mārauñ	māriuñ	mārenhi	mārinhi, mārīñ
2d "	māresi, mārehi, māreu, māraū	mārisi, māriu	mārehu	mārihu
3d "	māresi, mārehi, māreu, māraū	mārisi, māriu	mārenhi	mārinhi, mārīñ

It is probable, although there is much confusion in the use of these terminations, that in the 1st sing. *-uñ* represents *amhi*, *-si* in the 2d sing. *asi*, and *-nhi* in the 1st and 3d plur. *amho* or *ahanti*. Traces of this tense are found, but with *neuter* verbs only, in Chand (as *bulliva* = Rām. *boleu*, *bhrameva* = *bhrameu*).

The Sanskrit *future participle passive* in *-itavya* in Prākrit ends in *-idavva*, *-iavva*, *-ibba*; thus Sk. *karitavya* (for the classical *kartavya*) is in Pk. *karidavva, kariavva, karibba*. No trace of this participle exists in High Hindī; but in the dialects it has yielded (1) a gerund or verbal noun, which will be noticed hereafter; and (2) a future, which is used throughout all the Eastern Hindī area in the present day, and is frequent in the *Rāmāyan*. Just as in the eastern country the past participle passive lost its passive sense and had added to it fragments of the present tense of √*as* to make an active past, so the future passive participle has, in precisely the same region and in that only, lost its passive sense and had added to it a similar set of terminations to make an active future. The tendency of these much abraded terminations, which we are led by analogy to connect with the substantive verb, to disappear altogether is well illustrated by the future in the *Rāmāyan*, which ends for all persons in both numbers in *-aba*, *iba*, although in the modern dialects of Oudh, Rīwāñ, and Bhojpur fuller forms survive. The following is the scheme of the eastern future in *-ba* :—

		Awadhi.	*Riwāī.*	*Rāmāyan.*	*Bengali future.*
Sing.	1st pers.	mārabūñ	mārabyeuñ	māriba, māraba	māriba
	2d "	mārabes, mārabe	māribes	"	māribi
	3d "	(wanting)	(wanting)	"	māribe
Plur.	1st "	māraba	māribai	"	māriba
	2d "	mārabo	māribā	"	māribā
	3d "	(wanting)	(wanting)	"	māriben

There are two other types of the future in Hindī which, though not participial tenses of the same kind as those just noticed, may conveniently be considered here. The first is that in use in the standard dialect, which is formed by adding to the present the terminations *-gā*, *-ge*, for the masc. sing. and plur., and *-gī*, *-gīñ*, for the fem. (in Braj *-gau*, *-gai*, *-gī*, in Kanaujī *-go*, *-ge*, *-gī*).

This type is the common future in Panjābī, and is alone employed in the present day in Western Hindī; in the older authors it is of comparatively rare occurrence, though it is certainly ancient, occurring in Nāmdeo, the *Rāmāyan*, and Kabīr. There is little doubt that the *-gā* added to the present in this form of the future is the past participle of √*gam*, "to go," identical with the modern *gayā* (which is not seldom in the poets contracted to *gau*, *ga*, as *bhayā* is to *bhau*, *bha*) ; *mārūñ-gā* would then literally mean—"I am gone that I may beat," = "I am going to beat," or "I will beat."

The other form is used in Rājpūtānā and the Himālayan dialects of Kumāun, Gaṛhwāl, and Nepāl. It is exactly parallel to the *gā*-form, except that instead of *gā* it adds to the terminations of the present *lā* (*lo*), &c. *L* is also the characteristic termination of the future in Marāthī. It seems probable that in this affix we have the past participle *lagā*, reduced to *laā*, *lā*, from the verb *lag*, "begin."

c. *The Compound Tenses.*—These are formed by adding to the participles discussed in the previous section various tenses of auxiliary verbs ; they differ from the simply participial tenses in that the latter consist either of participles alone, or have incorporated in them and no longer separable only fragmentary remnants of the verb √*as* ; while in the compound tenses each element has a separate and independent form, which can if necessary be placed apart in the sentence from its fellow. The tenses so formed are numerous, and sometimes express very fine shades of meaning ; they have grown up for the most part out of modern needs and strivings after precision, and, though extremely interesting when considered from the logical side of grammar, are not so instructive with reference to the historical development of the language as those described in the two preceding sections. It will therefore suffice to mention briefly the auxiliaries which are used to form these tenses, and to exhibit in a few types their construction.

Descendants of the following Sanskrit and Prākrit roots are used as auxiliaries in Hindī and its dialects :—(1) √*as* ; (2) √*achchh* ; (3) √*vṛit* ; (4) √*sthā* ; (5) √*rah* ; (6) √*bhū*. √*Yā* is sometimes counted as an auxiliary verb used to form the passive ; but it is in this use more properly regarded as an ancillary, and has already been treated above.

√*As* yields the simple present in Hindī; which in the classical language takes the form—sing., 1st pers. *hauñ*, *hūñ*, 2d pers. *hai*, 3d pers. *hai* ; plur., 1st pers. *haiñ*, 2d pers. *ho*, 3d pers. *haiñ*. In the older language the following fuller forms are met with :—

	Singular.	*Plural.*
1st pers.	ahauñ	ahahiñ, ahaïñ, hahiñ
2d „	ahasi, ahahi, āhi, ahaï, ahai	ahahu, hahu
3d „	ahahi, āhi, ahaï, ahai	ahahiñ, āhaiñ, ahaïñ, hahiñ

These forms take us back, according to the principles of derivation already set forth, to a Sanskrit and Prākrit tense which should exhibit the following scheme :—

Sanskrit.

Sing., 1st pers. asāmi ; 2d pers. asasi ; 3d pers. asati.
Plur., 1st pers. asāmah ; 2d pers. asatha (asadhwam) ; 3d pers. asanti

Prākrit.

Sing., 1st pers. ahami ; 2d pers. ahasi ; 3d pers. ahaï
Plur., 1st pers. ahamha ; 2d pers. ahahu ; 3d pers. ahanti

Such a tense would result from conjugating √*as* according to the *bhū*-form ; and we have seen that all Sanskrit roots as a rule take this form, whatever their conjugation in Sanskrit, in Prākrit. But the root *as* in the latter language is an exception, the forms being derived direct from the Sanskrit tense, which follows the *ad*-conjugation—Sk. asmi, asi, asti, smah, stha, santi; Pk. amhi, asi, atthi, amha, attha, santi. It seems beyond doubt that we are justified in assuming, although no specimens of such a tense have yet been found in literary Prākrit, that it did exist in the popular language and has been the parent, first of the archaic, and then of the modern Hindī.

This auxiliary is used with the present participle to form an absolute present, as *dekhtā hai*, "he is seeing;" and with the past participle to form an absolute past, as *us-ne dekhā hai*, "he has seen." Besides this much used present tense, some have referred to the root *as* the Braj and Māṛwāṛī past participle (used as a past tense), masc. *ho*, plur. *he*, fem. *hī*, plur. *hīñ*; this may have come from a past participle *asitah*, through a Prākrit form *ahio*, *ahiao*, possible early Hindī *ahyau*, *aho*; it seems, however, more probable that *ho* is to be connected with *thā* (to which it corresponds) by the passage of *th* into *h*. Another participle used to form a past in Kanaujī is *hato*, plur. *hate*, fem. *hatī*, plur. *hatīñ*; this is most probably from the Sanskrit pres. participle *asan*, Pk. *asanto*, *ahanto*, *ahantao*, Hindī *ahatau*, *hato*. The change of meaning with this participle from present to past has parallels in other Indo-Aryan languages. The present participle *santo* is also used in Eastern Hindī in the inflected form for *hote* in the locative absolute, as—yah asakya sante, "this being impossible."

√*Achchh* is a root not found in classical Sanskrit, but common in Prākrit in the sense of *standing*, *being*, *existing*. It has been supposed by some that it is a modification of √*as*, and by others that it is the Prākrit form of the Sanskrit √*aksh*. It is not used in High Hindī, but is largely employed in substitution for the auxiliaries derived from √*as* in Mewāṛī, the Himālayan dialects, Tirhūtī, and the Dakhnī dialect of Urdū; in Oṛiyā and Bengali it is the common auxiliary, and is also much used in Marāṭhī under the form *as* (*ch* and *chh* becoming *s* in that dialect). In all the Hindī dialects but Dakhnī it has lost its initial vowel, which is retained in Bengali, Oṛiyā, and Marāṭhī. The following tenses of it are found in Hindī :—

Present ("I am," &c.)

	Singular.			*Plural.*		
	1st pers.	2d pers.	3d pers.	1st pers.	2d pers.	3d pers.
Kumāunī	chhyauñ	chhai	chha	chhoñ	chhā	chhan, chhīñ
Gaṛhwālī	chhauñ	chhai	chha	chhauñ	chhan	chhan
Mewāṛī	chhūñ	chhai	chhai	chhāñ	chho	chhai

Past (properly a participle = "I was," &c.): *Kumāunī*, sing. masc. chhiyo, plur. masc. chhiyā; *Mewāṛī*, chho, chhā; *Gaṛhwālī* has a different root for this tense.

√*Vrit* is found as an auxiliary in substitution for √*as* in the Awadhī and Bhojpurī dialects; the following forms are in use—*Awadhī*, sing., 1st pers. bāṭyeuñ, 2d pers. bāṭe, 3d pers. bāṭai;

plur., 1st pers. bāṭī, 2d pers. bāṭyo, bāṭyeñ, 3d pers. bāṭaiñ; *Bhojpurī* has bāte, bate for all persons in both numbers. These forms are from the Śanskrit present ātmanepada *vartate*, &c., through the Prākrit *vaṭṭaï*. It is probably to this stem (and not to √*bhū*) that we must refer the indeclinable *bā*, much used throughout the Eastern Hindī area as far west as Allahabad, and the Bhojpurī forms (used in questions and answers) *bārīñ* (1st sing. and plur.), *bāra* (2d sing. and plur.), *bāran* (3d sing. and plur.).

√*Sthā* has yielded the common past participial auxiliary in Hindī, sing. masc. *thā*, plur. *the*, fem. *thī*, plur. *thīñ*, used with present and past participles thus—maiñ dekhtā thā, "I was seeing;" maiñ-ne dekhā thā, "I had seen." *Thā* is from *sthitah*, as is proved by its forms in Nepālī and Gaṛhwālī; in the former it makes, with incorporation of the substantive verb, a regular participial tense,—sing., 1st pers. *thiyāñ*, 2d pers. *this*, 3d pers. *thiyā*; plur., 1st pers. *thiyuñ*, 2d pers. *thiyau*, 3d pers. *thiyā*. The Gaṛhwālī form is *thayo*, masc. sing., *thayā*, masc. plur., *thaī*, fem. sing. and plur.

The past participle of the stem *rah* (in the Hindī sense of "to remain") is used in the Eastern dialects (Awadhī, Riwāī, Bhojpurī, Tirhūtī, and the language of the Rāmāyan) as a substitute for *thā* to form a past tense; as—jo kachhu uchita rahā so kīnhā = High Hindī—jo kuchh uchit thā so kiyā.

There is yet another auxiliary used in place of √*as* to form a present in Gaṛhwāl, viz., sing., all persons, *lo*; plur., all persons, *lā*; as—koī lo? = High Hindī—koī hai? Tuin auñdā lā = H. H. tum āte ho. The derivation of this word has not yet been explained.

The root *bhū* is one of great importance in the modern languages, as it is chiefly by its means that the more elaborate modifications of tense and mood are effected. The auxiliaries hitherto discussed express only simple present and past time; derivatives of *bhū* are used, either alone or together with these auxiliaries, to express probability, conditional existence, continuance, commencement, and various other secondary shades of meaning. In standard Hindī this root assumes the form *ho*, derived from the Sk. present bhavati, Pk. hodi, hoï; but it has in the dialects an old tadbhava past participle in which the *bh* survives, bhayā, by the side of huā (from Sk. bhūtah, Pk. huo); the former is from a formation in *-ita*, bhavitah, which would in Prākrit be bhaïo. In the dialects also the stem *ho* frequently hardens the vowel to *w*, assuming the form *hwai*, *hwe*. Of this root we have the following tenses in common use; (1) a present, *howe*; (2) an imperative, *ho*; (3) a future, *hogā* (dial. *hosī*, *hwesī*, *hwaihai*, *hoiahi*, *hob*, *hoilo*); (4) a passive or respectful imperative *hūje*, *hūjiye*; (5) a present participle *hotā* (dial. *howantu*, *hūnta*, *hotu*, *hot*, *hotau*); (6) a past participle, *bhayā*, *huā* (dial. *bhayau*, *bhayaū*, *bhā*, *bhaila*); besides various tenses made by combining with these the other auxiliaries. To this root also apparently belongs a Braj past tense *hutau* (*-e*, *-ī*), used as a substitute for *thā*, which is probably from the Pk. pres. part.

huvanto, huvantao, which occurs in Old Hindī under the form *hūnta* as a past tense. Of the six forms above given, the present, future, and present participle are constantly used as auxiliaries, the rest chiefly as independent tenses.

Lastly, the verb *karnā*, "to do," is much used in rustic Eastern Hindī to form periphrastic tenses with the gerund, where in the standard dialect a form of the verb itself would be employed. The gerund which appears in this idiom is that derived from the Sk. future passive participle, ending in the nom. in *-ibo*, oblique *-ibe*, and the construction is most common in negative sentences.

d. *Other Verbal Forms.*—Under this head it will suffice to mention (1) the conjunctive participle, (2) the infinitive or gerund, and (3) the noun of agency.

The *conjunctive participle* in standard Hindī appears either under the form of the verbal stem only (as *mār, chal* = "having beaten," "having gone"), or more commonly under that of the stem increased by the addition of *kar, ke, karke,* or *karkar*; as *mārkar, chalke, uṭhkarke, sunkarkar.* It is very much used to link together subordinate clauses in narration, and forms one of the chief features of the Indian as opposed to the English syntax. This construction, like that of the agent and the passive participle, is a survival from Sanskrit and Prākrit. In archaic Hindī this participle ends in *-i*, as *māri, kari, suni*, and when the root ends in a long vowel, sometimes in *-e*, as *khāe, pāe, bulāe, jāe.* In Chand a still longer form, in *iya*, is found. It corresponds to the Prākrit conjunctive participle in *-ia*, as karia, sunia, which are in Sanskrit kṛitwā, śrutwa. In the latter language this participle takes both the terminations *-ya* and *-twā*, the former chiefly in compound roots and the latter in simple ones; but in the northern Prākrits the former, resolved to *-ia*, is alone used. A survival of the Sanskrit *-twā* is, however, found in Māṛwāṛī, where the conjunctive participle ends in *-ūne* (marūne, sunūne, &c.); this represents the Prākrit *-ūna*, formed from the Sanskrit *-twānam*, accusative of *-twā*, by the loss of the *t* and vocalization of the *w*; as Sk. mṛitwā, Pk. maraūna, Māṛwāṛī marūne. The affix *kar* (older *kari*) is itself the conjunctive participle of *karnā*, and was added when, owing to the loss of the final *-i*, the verbal root only remained, and need was felt of greater distinctness.

The conjunctive participle is not only much used as a connective for the members of a sentence, but in composition with ancillary verbs forms a vast number of compounds, the nature of which is clear from the older forms of the language, in which the first member always appear with the final *-i* or *iya.* In these the idea of separate action contained in the participle has been lost, and the two words express only one act. Such words are *le-ānā* (contracted *lānā*), "to bring" (lit., "having taken to come"); *khā-jānā*, "to eat up" (lit., "having eaten to go"); *pī-lenā*, "to drink down"; *pheṅk-denā*, "to throw away," &c.

The modern *infinitive* is really a gerund, the Sanskrit infinitive in *-tum* having entirely disappeared. It ends in the standard dialect in *-nā*, inflected *-ne*, fem. *-nī*, plur. *-nīṅ*. In the dialects it has two forms, of one of which the characteristic letter is *n*, of the other *w* or *b*. To the first class belong Kanaujī *mārno*, *māran*, Rāmāyan *māran*, Braj *mārnauñ* (inflected *mārani*), Rājpūtānā *mārṇo*, *mārṇūñ*, Bhojpuri *mārnāñ*; to the second Braj *māriwauñ*, Rājpūtānā *mārabo*, Awadhī, Riwāī, and Rāmāyan *mārab*. Of these forms the first has been shown by Dr Hoernle[1] to be derived from the Sanskrit future passive participle in *-anīyam*, which became in Prākrit *-aṇiam*, *-aṇaam*, and in Braj *-anauñ* (where the anuswāra characteristic of the Prākrit neuter has, as usual, yielded anunāsika and a labial vowel). The second is a descendant of the future passive participle in *-itavyam*, Pk. *idavvam*, *iavvam*, *ibbam*, and with the *k*-augment *-ibbaam*, whence Braj *-iwauñ*, Māṛwāṛī *-ibo*. The participial origin of these infinitives is proved, not only by phonetic probabilities, but by two peculiar constructions common in Hindī. The first is that in which the infinitive varies in gender with the conjoined noun. The second is the very frequent use of the infinitive as an imperative, as — aisā kām kabhī na karnā, "never do such a thing"; which is explicable only by referring to the original sense of *karnā* = *karaṇīyam*, the literal translation of the phrase being—" such a thing is never to be done." Similarly, the infinitive is used passively in such phrases as—tum-ko wahāñ jānā hai, "you must go there," lit., "for you there it is to be gone," *tibi eundum est*, where necessity is implied in the future passive participle. The transition from a future passive to a present active sense has an exact parallel in the Latin gerund, where, while *amandus* means "to be loved," *in amando* means "in loving."

The *noun of agency* is formed by adding to the inflected infinitive the affixes *wālā* and *hārā*, as *karne-wālā*, "doer," *gāne-hārā* "singer." Of these the former probably represents the Sk. *pālakah*, Pk. *vālao*, and the latter the Sk. *dhārakah*, Pk. *hārao*.

Bibliography.—The study of Hindī and its sisters from the historical point of view is very recent, and much still remains to be done. The first foundations were laid in Dr E. Trumpp's *Sindhī Grammar* (1872), which treated incidentally of the other allied Indian vernaculars. Almost simultaneously appeared the first three of Dr Hoernle's valuable *Essays on the Gauṛian Languages* (*J. A. S. B.*, 1872, 1873, 1874), and the first volume of Mr Beames's *Comparative Grammar of the Modern Aryan Languages of India* (vol. i. 1872; vol. ii. 1875; vol. iii. 1879). Dr Hoernle's essays at present (October 1879) go no further than the declension of nouns. Mr Beames's work covers the whole ground, but is naturally more thorough and satisfactory in the later portions than in the earlier. Mr Kellogg's admirable *Hindī Grammar* (Allahabad, 1876) is our sole authority on most of the Hindī dialects, and is exhaustive in all that concerns the Braj-bhākhā and the Old Pūrbī of the *Rāmāyan*. Dr Trumpp's introduction and notes to his *Translation of the Ādi Granth* (1877) contain much valuable matter; but the author has preferred to reserve a complete discussion of the language of this, the most valuable store of Old Hindī, for a separate work, the early appearance of which is promised. Of Hindustani grammars, not dealing specially with the historical development of the language, the best are perhaps those of Professor Monier Williams, Professor Dowson (London, 1872), and Mr Platts (London, 1874). Of Dakhnī-Urdū little has been written; a short sketch of its forms was appended to the 4th edition of Shakespear's *Hindustani Grammar* (1843). Mr Kellogg's work renders reference to other Hindī grammars needless.

---

[1] *J. A. S. B.*, 1873, pt. i. p. 66 *sqq*.